GW01080932

Dear Thea,

YOU'RE AWESOME

Living a Fulfilled Life

Di Smith

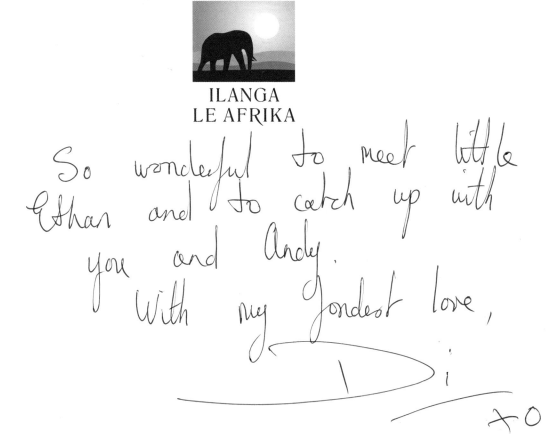

**ILANGA
LE AFRIKA**

So wonderful to meet little
Ethan and to catch up with
you and Andy.
With my fondest love,

Di
xo

YOU'RE AWESOME
Living a Fulfilled Life

Published in 2011 by Awesome SA Publishers.

ADDRESS:
P.O. Box 13111, Cascades
Pietermartizburg, 3202
KwaZulu-Natal, South Africa

E-mail: di@awesomesa.co.za
Website: www.awesomesa.co.za

ISBN:
978-0-620-49440-3 soft cover
978-0-620-49441-0 hard cover

© Di Smith 2011
Copyright for the photographs remains with Terrence Mtola

Photographs: Terrence Mtola
Editor: Moray Comrie
Layout and design: Marise and Candy Bauer, M Design
Printed by Interpak Books and Distributed by Blue Weaver
The photograph of Nelson Mandela was kindly supplied by Siphiwe Mhlambi –
African Skies Media – 082 554 4184

All rights reserved. Apart from any fair dealing for the purpose of private study, research, criticism or review, as permitted under the Copyright Act, no part may be reproduced by any process without written permission. Enquiries should be made to the publisher.

All effort has been made to uphold the copyright of any of the quotes or material reproduced in this compilation. In cases where there might have been an oversight and copyright permission was not granted by the rightful owner, the publisher would be pleased to receive the relevant information to make amendments in future editions.

There is a destiny that makes us brothers —

None goes his way alone:

All that which we send into the lives of others,

Comes back into our own

– Edwin Markham
(Writer and poet: 1852–1940)

Contents

Foreword
by Archbishop Emeritus Desmond Tutu

Nobel Peace Prize Laureate

I have a firm conviction that we are made for goodness out of goodness. But how do we achieve goodness when it becomes buried under our faults and failures?

We all have choices. We can live a life of significance or move on from this world without having achieved our full potential. We are created to be so much more than we realise. Through our choices we can let the lure of things that are not wholesome turn us away from the goodness within us, or we can make the choice to act on our deep-rooted knowledge of that which is good.

In this book, Di Smith has woven the timeless wisdom of great thinkers together with practical steps drawn from her own everyday experience. If we have the will and determination to change for the better, we can apply these to transform our own lives and influence the lives of others around us as we live into the goodness which is our essence.

Introduction

I am a child of Africa. I grew up among the Xhosa people on our family farm in South Africa.

Willowdale Farm lies at the foot of Diamond Hill in a magnificent area of KwaZulu-Natal called East Griqualand. The roots of my family tree lie deep in the soil of Africa, having been planted by successive family members of bygone generations.

When you have been born in Africa the rhythms of the continent pulse within your blood, and no matter the colour of your skin, you are marked by Africa and linked to all her peoples by a shared spirit. You have an African soul.

Africa, the cradle of mankind, has been distilled throughout the ages. It is the continent of poetry, music, dance and *Ubuntu*, and holds unequalled wisdom and dignity in those areas which have not been marred by ruthless plunder, power, greed and disregard for others.

My own love for this country grew out of my childhood days, roaming free on horseback or on foot. My early morning call was the rising sun and my night time memories are of star filled skies stretching to the horizon and a deep still silence broken only by the sound of nocturnal creatures. Nature was my greatest teacher. I learned at an early age the natural rhythms of life and death, joy and sorrow, the change of the seasons and the progression of youth to old age.

My childhood was happy and secure and it was then that I developed the respect and love I have for Africa and its people.

Human folly and disregard for its people and wildlife has been part of Africa's evolution. Conquest became the symbol of Africa, from the time that it was still ruled by its indigenous people to the slave trade under Arab occupation and then the grabbing of almost the whole continent by foreign invaders.

Africa was carved up by the great European powers who disregarded existing tribal and racial boundaries. Just as with her natural environment of bush, swamp, grassland and desert, her history has been filled with extremes. Today dire poverty and untold wealth vie for domination of this vast and beautiful continent.

Perhaps the suffering of the past has prepared the people of Africa for a greater purpose.

South Africa, at the southernmost tip of the continent, is the one country that gives hope to Africa and indeed the whole world.

The peaceful transition from apartheid to democracy was led by a great man, Nelson Mandela, whose strength and dignity paved the way into a new era.

Archbishop Emeritus Desmond Tutu, the conscience of our nation, never doubted the power of reconciliation. He has repeatedly called for South Africans to practise *Ubuntu*. Archbishop Tutu defines *Ubuntu* in two parts. "The first is that the person is friendly, hospitable, generous, gentle, caring and compassionate. In other words, someone who will use their strengths on behalf of others – the weak and the poor and the ill – and not take advantage of anyone. This person treats others as he would like to be treated. And because of this they express the second part of the concept which concerns openness, large-heartedness. They share their worth."

In practising the qualities of *Ubuntu*, the person's humanity is affirmed, both for the giver and the receiver.

The Truth and Reconciliation Commission, led by Archbishop Tutu, helped South Africa on the road to healing and into a new democracy by providing a platform for both the previously oppressed and the former oppressors to regain their dignity and humanity. The Truth and Reconciliation Commission underscores the importance of consensus and agreement and reconciliation. This work needs to be carried forward by the people of this incredible country. The work is ongoing!

It is time for the winds of change again to blow over a continent that has had more than its fair share of atrocities and oppression driven by the greed for money and power.

I have an African vision that I long to see fulfilled.

I dream that the dignity and nobility of the African people that is inherent in their tradition will surface once again in our society, particularly in those areas where corruption and the unwholesome grasping for materialism and power, disregarding all others, has become entrenched.

I dream of a society where every single person matters, where families are united, where communities live with strong spiritual principles, where every child is nurtured and educated, and where people make the right choices and live their lives with integrity.

I dream that people will live without discrimination and with acceptance for those who are different from themselves in colour, culture and religion.

I dream that we shall make peace with the past and that every individual will play a part in the ongoing work of reconciliation through the principles of *Ubuntu*.

I dream that the dark clouds that for so long have covered the African continent will lift and that the light that shines through will give an unequalled nobility and dignity to the people of this great continent.

I dream that Africa will lead the way in living consciously, and create a new world order in the way we live our lives.

My own love affair with Africa has prompted the writing of this book. I dream that within its pages the calling to greatness will awaken in each one of us. I dream that through this awakening we will walk together into the future and create the country and ultimately the continent that we have it in us to become.

Acknowledgements

I could not possibly name all the people and books that have had a profound influence on me during my life. I would like to express my deep gratitude to those who have shared their messages of wisdom with humanity over the ages and particularly to those whose work has influenced the writing of this book.

I dedicate this book to the following people.

Nelson Mandela and Archbishop Emeritus Desmond Tutu for embracing *Ubuntu* and being such great examples to the people of South Africa and mankind.

Terrence Mtola for your photographs which depict the beauty of our people and the magnificence of our country.

Stephanie Alexander for your help and encouragement when I took my first faltering steps towards the writing of this book.

Derryn Campbell, friend, colleague and co-founder of Awesome SA, who self-published her first book, *Awesome South Africa*, ahead of me and thus was able to assist me in bringing this book to publication.

Nosipo Mgojo and Sandra Holley for your infectious enthusiasm and commitment to transforming the lives of others.

Karen Lotter and Geraldine Somerset for your unwavering support, assistance and friendship.

Marguerite Poland, Pippa Wood, Judy Wintgens, Gcina Mhlophe, Nana Ngobese and Brad Butler for reading through the first draft of this book and giving sound advice and encouragement.

Moray Comrie, my editor, whose creativity and command of the English language has directed this book to completion.

Marise and Candice Bauer, for your commitment to excellence.

Love and thanks to my parents, Jack and Joan Bastard, whose values and integrity moulded my life and those of my siblings, Mary, Helen, Val and Max: and especially to my husband Guy and our three children, Candice, Paul and Matt. You have been my greatest teachers.

I would also like to thank the people of South Africa whose courage and dedication to the life-transforming vision for freedom has and continues to move our country forward.

How to use this book to find the miracle of life and dance to your own rhythm

If we view life as a dance and the events and people we encounter as our dancing partners, then we need to learn the steps of the dance so that our lives become gracious and complete. From our arrival in the world until our departure from it, having someone show us the steps can prevent us from stumbling and falling. Desmond Tutu in his book *Believe* says that "None of us comes into the world fully formed. We would not know how to think, or walk or speak or behave as human beings unless we learned it from other human beings". The material in this book shows steps we can learn to lead fuller, happier and more fulfilling lives and if we do falter, the means to get up and move forward again.

The material is presented in 52 chapters, one for each week of the year so that the book could be studied and worked with over a period of a year.

You could use the book in any of the following ways:

1. Skim through the book rapidly at first to get an overall view of it, marking the chapters that have special appeal, returning to work on them later.

2. Work systematically through the whole book, chapter by chapter, analysing where each principle can be applied in your life.

3. Apply the lessons from each chapter to your life for a week before moving onto the following chapter.

If you wish to get the most out of this book there is one essential requirement – a deep, driving desire to learn and the determination to apply these principles daily. The only way to learn and improve is by doing. Genuine change does not happen overnight. Good behaviour patterns come step by step with gradual familiarisation. Use these principles at every opportunity. By continually self-analysing and applying the principles to your life on a daily basis, you will discover your true self and will be on the road to contentment and happiness.

CHAPTER 1

Learn to Be Silent

"Silence is the music of your soul and the road to inner peace is by dancing to your own song."

— Anonymous

Through the normal emotional ups and downs of adolescence, I would often saddle up my horse and ride off into the hills. I was always amazed at the way in which, when on my own with nature, my feelings of resentment and anger would disappear. It was only in later years, living in a city, that I came to understand how this contact with nature enabled me to find inner peace by sensing the unity of all of life within the vastness of the African veld.

Modern living, especially in cities, is filled with "busy-ness" and noise. Life can become overwhelming when we do not find time to quiet our mind, connect to our inner voice and refresh our soul.

My quiet time sets the tone for my day, whether it is reading to re-kindle my spirit, sitting in silent meditation and prayer, or communing with nature where I sense the harmonious interaction of all of life. During this time I reconnect to that part of myself, my inner voice, that can so easily be lost in the rush of modern day living.

We need to take time-out from our frenetic lives and be still. If you are unable to get into a garden or the countryside, then sit quietly and watch a sunset or listen to the sound of the rain on the roof or the wind outside.

*"When you lose
touch with
stillness,
you lose touch
with yourself.
When you lose
touch with
yourself,
you lose touch
with the world."*

– Eckhart Tolle

It was the Austro-Hungarian writer, Franz Kafka, who said, "You need not leave your room. Remain sitting at your table and just listen. You need not even listen, simply wait. You need not even wait; just learn to become quiet, and still, and solitary. The world will freely offer itself to you to be unmasked. It has no choice; it will roll in ecstasy at your feet".

Experiencing solitude and silence every day will keep you centred on your life goals and plugged into your intuition and your inner voice.

Psalm 46:10 reads "Be still and know that I am God" – for it is only in stillness, when every other voice is hushed that you can hear the voice from within: the authentic voice of the soul. During your quiet time, your mind needs to be guided away from the many thoughts that come and go. Withdraw your mind inward by focusing your attention simply on your breathing. Become aware of inhaling and exhaling. By following the pattern of your breath your mind will settle and become still.

Create a "sacred space" and, at a similar time each day, take time for yourself. Switch off the chatter for a while and be still, be silent.

In your daily life, when you have once again stepped into busyness, carry your stillness within you. It will guide you through your waking hours and you will not be overshadowed by the chaos of life around you.

CHAPTER 2

Smile and Say Hello

"Too often we underestimate the power of a touch, a smile, a kind word,
a listening ear, an honest compliment, or the smallest act of caring,
all of which have the potential to turn a life around."

– *Leo Buscaglia*

Have you ever had a stranger smile and say hello?

Have you felt how it lifts your spirit and makes you feel worthy and accepted?

It is extremely difficult not to reciprocate with a smile and a greeting when someone warmly says hello.

Say hello to people who are outside your circle of family and friends. Step away from your fears and replace them with the simple act of saying hello.

"What does the colour of one's skin tell us that is of any significance about a person? Nothing, of course, absolutely nothing. It does not say whether the person is warm-hearted or kind, clever or witty, or whether that person is good." – Desmond Tutu.

There is something great in everyone. Find the time to get to know someone who is out of your social circle.

Start a conversation with someone who comes from a different background and you will be encouraged to discover how much you have in common. You will be surprised to find that you may come to like them or even love them.

Make your day worthwhile by brightening the day of just one other person.

CHAPTER 3

Accept Yourself

"This above all: to thine own self be true,
And it must follow, as the night the day,
Thou canst not then be false to any man."

— William Shakespeare

Many people today do not accept themselves.

"If only I were more beautiful."

"If only I had more money."

"If only I had married someone else."

If only, if only, if only. They live their lives with regret.

If you do not love yourself first, you are incapable of loving others, for you have nothing to give.

The media influence us powerfully. The media dictate what we should look like, feel like, and how we should live. It is impossible to do and be all these things, and at the end of the day it really does not matter.

We are all unique with unique looks and talents. There has never been anyone on this earth who is exactly like you and there never will be again. You are one of a kind.

There is great wisdom in the words "lose yourself to find yourself" for no matter where you go, you will always be accompanied by yourself, so get to know and like that person.

If you have regrets about being you, then the road to self-love is to shift your focus from yourself to others. By serving and reaching out to other people, you will grow in self-confidence, self-belief and self-love. Concentrate on helping the people around you and you will find your own happiness and a sense of well-being.

Poise and self-confidence are available to each one of us. Each of us in our own way has to find the place where we can do life's ordinary things in a manner that touches others and moves them to do great things with their own lives.

CHAPTER 4

Make Wise Choices

"It is not wealth one asks for, but just enough to preserve one's dignity,
to work unhampered, to be generous, frank and independent."
– W. Somerset Maugham

Sikhumbuzo Mhlongo, a young South African, committed suicide because he could not get an identity document (ID), which he needed to get employment. Every citizen over the age of 18 must present an ID document for just about every official business transaction – opening a bank account, applying for a passport, getting a driver's licence, finding employment and so on. Unfortunately, many people have experienced great difficulties and delays in obtaining these documents.

Sikhumbuzo wrote in his suicide note, "I have persevered too long. I have lost my job because my ID was turned down. It hurts to see my friends go to work. I don't want to steal. I prefer to die than to go to jail".

Sikhumbuzo wanted nothing more than to live his life with dignity by working so that he could hold his head high. This was denied him by the inhumane way he was treated by officials. Archbishop Desmond Tutu reinforces this with his words "We humans can tolerate suffering but we cannot tolerate meaninglessness".

Bhikkhu Bodhi, an American born Buddhist Monk, defined living with dignity as follows: "To live with dignity means to be one's own master: to conduct one's affairs on the basis of one's own free choices instead of being pushed around by forces beyond one's control".

To live with dignity means you put your worth as a human being above the conscious pursuit of wealth, power and fame.

Human beings are the only living organism with the capacity for moral choice. Although your choices are limited to a certain extent by your surroundings, you have an inner freedom that allows you to choose to change yourself and thereby change the world. The choices you make are in every moment and the road you take depends on you. All the choices you have

"No race can prosper till it learns that there is as much dignity in tilling a field as in writing a poem."

– Booker T Washington

made in the past have resulted in what is happening in your life at the present moment.

You are free to choose to rise to the heights of spiritual greatness or to sink to degrading depths. It's up to you. Your intuition or inner voice will guide you in making the correct choice in every moment. The decision that is right is the decision which leaves you with a feeling of warmth and well-being.

Dignity is closely connected with self-discipline. Self-discipline gives you freedom from the temptations of passion and prejudice. You draw your strength from within, guided by your knowledge of truth and the correct choice in any given moment. Drawing on your inner strength enables you to turn away from frivolous self-indulgence and the disregard for human dignity in yourself and in others.

The decisions you make count and have consequences that extend far beyond themselves. Your choices will determine your long-term suffering or your own happiness.

South African author Emmaleen Kriel has written a book called *Close the Door Softly Behind You*. The story is her foray into the world of manual labour and how it brings new insight and appreciation for those in domestic service. She writes a letter of apology to all the maids she has known and gives grateful thanks for their loyal service. This book reminds us to treat people from any walk of life with dignity.

CHAPTER 5

Write a Journal

"Be yourself. Above all, let who you are, what you are, what you believe,
shine through every sentence you write, every piece you finish."

— John Jakes

At one time I decided to start an export business because the South African currency was so weak. Shortly after this, the Rand strengthened and exporting from South Africa to the United States became unprofitable. I lost quite a sum of money in this enterprise, which was the third small business I had started and the first to fail. I felt devastated. I needed to come to terms with the monetary loss and the sense of failure.

At about the same time my youngest son, Matt, was about to turn 21. I decided to put together a journal of his life. I rummaged through all the books, certificates, cards and school work that I had kept for all those years. I sifted through all our family photographs. My mind became filled with memories of our years together as a family. I wrote, drew, stuck in photos and cards and eventually gave this to him from our family as our gift for his coming of age.

What surprised me was that the exercise was cathartic for me personally, helping me cope with my failure.

The easiest path to come to terms with the past and find peace is through writing. Writing a journal or scrap booking is a healthy release in dealing with emotions such as distress and grief. It helps to put things into perspective. It allows you the opportunity to find your inner healing without having to turn to others. It will give you a sense of empowerment. Writing opens the door to your unconscious mind and allows creativity to visit you.

Writing in your journal does not have to be done every day but when you do write, set aside at least twenty minutes to express your feelings. Just jotting down a few pointers does not have the benefits of concentrated writing, which is like having a one-to-one conversation with yourself.

A journal should not just be a record of the day-to-day events in your life. It should be about what you achieved during the day, your experiences, thoughts and feelings.

Write down what made you laugh, what made you cry, those things for which you are grateful. Write down the compliments or criticism, as well as your reactions of being thrilled, proud or disappointed. You will find the situations that stick most in your mind are the ones that touched you emotionally.

The best way to start a journal is simply to write down all the events during your day that made you laugh. The surest way of releasing stress is to recall the jokes, the wisecracks of friends and your laughter.

Do not make your journal writing a chore. Keep a small pocket book to jot down reminders so that when it is convenient and you do sit down to write, you can recall the events and write down the accounts from your notes.

The aim of writing a journal is to evaluate and record events in your life. It is a place to learn from the experiences of your past, to keep a record of what you aim to do and why you want to do it. It is an outlet for your unconscious mind. Writing in your journal will enable you to grow in wisdom and assist you on your road to living a life of significance.

Writing is a powerful tool in developing self-awareness. Do not label the events you write about as right or wrong, they just are. Write about your emotions without feeling compelled to judge. A basic human need that we all share is the desire to be heard and understood. There are very few people who can hear us into healing without judging. Writing on the other hand gives you free rein for your feelings. It will define what is important in your life. It will clarify your feelings, your dreams and your aspirations.

There is no feeling, including the extremes of fear and grief, that does not find relief in writing.

CHAPTER 6

Conquer Your Fear

"It is not the critic who counts, nor the man who points out how the strong man stumbles or where the doer of deeds could have done better. The credit belongs to the man who is actually in the arena, whose face is marred by dust and sweat and blood; who knows great enthusiasm, great devotion and the triumph of achievement and who, at the worst, if he fails, at least fails while doing greatly — so that his place shall never be with those cold and timid souls who know neither victory nor defeat ...."

— Theodore Roosevelt

I stumbled across this quote in a book by Pete Goss called *Close to the Wind* when my children were in their teens. It is the story of a brave and compassionate man who gave up his position in a single-handed round-the-world-yacht race and turned into the teeth of a hurricane to save the life of a fellow competitor. I was so impressed with this story and the words by Theodore Roosevelt that I took the quote from the book and wrote them on cards, which I gave to my children as they left school. I told them that if they felt afraid to go out and try something, they should read these inspirational words.

What is failure?

Failure is the fact of being unable to do or become what is wanted, expected or attempted.

So often you dare not attempt to do what you would love to do because of the fear of failure. You imagine your unsuccessful attempt at doing something and visualise your world collapsing around you.

If you view failure as a gift which shapes your life and moulds your character then you will overcome the fear that pride creates around the myth of failure. Failure is a lesson learnt on your path to success.

Fear is the underlying emotion that holds us back from getting started. Every one of us faces fear. It not only comes as the fear of failure, but also the fear of change and the fear of success. Yes, believe it or not, many of us are afraid to succeed.

Did you know that more than 90% of perceived fears never materialise?

Archbishop Desmond Tutu explains fear as follows: "All of us experience fear but when we confront and acknowledge it we are able to turn it into courage. Being courageous does not mean never being scared; it means acting as you know you must even though you are undeniably afraid".

The way to overcome fear is to look it in the eye.

"You can conquer almost any fear if you will only make up your mind to do so. For remember, fear doesn't exist anywhere except in the mind." – Dale Carnegie

As soon as you decide not to attach importance to your failures, you are on the road to success. If you do fail on your first attempt, analyse the reasons for your failure, take corrective action and try again with more wisdom and renewed vigour.

You will succeed, if not the second time, then the third time.

It is wise to seek advice from those who have pursued a similar goal or have experience in that field. With perseverance you will overcome obstacles and gain more confidence and knowledge along the way.

Treat failures as steps towards success.

Nobody remembers the number of times you have failed, once you have succeeded.

It was Franklin D Roosevelt who said, "The only thing we have to fear is fear itself".

Replace your fears with faith in your capabilities, with faith in yourself and with faith in your ability to succeed. There is no failure if you keep trying until the day that you do succeed.

Every great musician has spent hours of practising; every great dancer has perfected a dance routine with time spent on the dance floor.

If you have failed more times than others, there is the very good chance that you have attempted to do more than others.

None of us wants to reach the end of our lives with the regret that we have let life slip by us.

Dale Carnegie summed it up in the following words: "Inaction breeds doubt and fear. Action breeds confidence and courage. If you want to conquer fear, do not sit home and think about it. Go out and get busy".

CHAPTER 7

Honour Your Family

"Trees are living symbols of peace and hope. A tree has roots in the soil yet reaches to the sky. It tells us that in order to aspire we need to be grounded and that no matter how high we go, it is from our roots that we draw sustenance. It is a reminder to all of us that have had success that we cannot forget where we came from."

– Wangari Maathai

Can you imagine your world without trees?

It would be desolate and barren.

You would have no oxygen to breathe or shade to cool you down.

Losing touch with your family and where you come from does the same to your spirit. You feel alone and desolate. You may be caught up in the dizziness of success but more than likely when the going gets tough, it will be your family that stands by you.

Do not push away those who really love and know you. You get most upset with those you love because they know your weaknesses. Make peace with your family and accept their inadequacies. You also have areas where you are vulnerable. We all do. As James McBride said, "It is the absurdity of family life, the raggedness of it, that is at once its redemption and its true nobility".

Acceptance simply means that you make a commitment to accept the people within your family. All families have their agreements and disagreements, but if we are strongly opposed to another family member's point of view, we need to sit and talk until we agree, so that we have a shared understanding.

A book I read as a girl – I no longer recall the title or author – told of a woman who was separated from her family in the Second World War and imprisoned in a concentration camp.

It was only once she no longer had a family to care for that she longed for the housework that she had slated. She ached to be reunited with her family and would have welcomed doing household chores for them.

So often you do not appreciate what you have until you no longer have it.

Plant a tree in gratitude for having a family with whom to share your life.

CHAPTER 8

Learn to Love the Early Morning

*"The miraculous beauty of a sunrise can only be appreciated
when we have risen in the dark."*

— Anonymous

On the farm where I grew up the pace of life was dictated to by the change of the seasons. Later I moved to the city.

As our children grew I found there were just not enough hours in the day to get through all that needed to be done and to meet the demands on my life. As a mother, wife and businesswoman, I made the decision to wake long before dawn so that I could have time to myself before the rest of the world woke up.

This has been one of the best decisions of my life and has transformed it, giving me the time to do all the things I love but for which I could never find the time.

By getting up early I have time to care for myself, and I have found that I could be a much better parent, wife and friend.

Not everyone likes the idea of rising early. Changing life habits can be difficult and disheartening but if you find that during the day you do not have time for yourself then do try getting up early. Give yourself a few weeks to allow this new habit to take hold. It will take effort and patience but by rising early and giving yourself your personal quiet time, the effort will be well worth it.

You will learn to love the peaceful early morning hours before sunrise. It is a time of new beginnings, the promise of a new day.

If you take the opportunity to set the tone for your day in these moments, you can build a reserve that will see you through your waking hours.

Listen to the sounds of nature greeting the new day. Life is a great gift. Cherish it with the renewal of every sunrise.

CHAPTER 9

Live in the Moment

"Look life straight in the eye, not to avoid it or wish it away. When we don't accept the true nature of our existence here then we find ourselves trying to control this tumbling universe to suit us, to make it predictable and safe, dodging the uncomfortable bits and holding on to the pieces we like. Attachment."

– Antony Osler

"Attachment" is defined as a connection or a bond that binds us to another person or a thing. We often think of "attachment" as keeping contact with good things in our lives – our home, our family, our friends and our possessions. When a person or object to which we are attached is no longer a part of our lives it leaves us with a feeling of negativity, as though a dark cloud is hanging over our heads.

The first time I became consciously aware of attachment and the need to let it go was when I realised that everything on earth exists in its own time.

I was conceived, I was born and I will also die when it is my time. Every day comes and every day goes, winter turns into spring, leaves drop from the trees to make way for the next spring, a precious object is dropped and shatters. So life goes on moment by moment.

If you are willing to let go of things that are comfortable, familiar and loved when they are no longer a part of your life then you will no longer be held back by a bundle of negative thoughts and emotions. You can move on with your life.

People and events come into your life for a reason, a lifetime or a season. You share, you learn and you grow. You laugh, you cry, you find peace, your get angry, you learn new things, you are complimented, you are criticised, you feel hurt, you feel joy, you love and are loved.

These are all normal human emotions. Everyone experiences them, moment by moment. If you accept people, circumstances and events as they come into your life and know that in every situation there is a lesson, then with this acceptance comes a quiet inner peace.

You learn to let go of endless frustration and anxiety by reminding yourself in every situation, "This moment is exactly as it should be". Remind yourself to not judge anything that occurs. With this awareness you will also relinquish the need to persuade others of your point of view and gain enormous amounts of energy that were previously wasted by the birth of an argument.

Give yourself completely to whatever is in front of you – the beauty of nature, the food you are preparing, every person you meet. If you live with awareness, the most mundane tasks can be fulfilling.

Listen to the Exhortation of the Dawn
Look to this Day!
For it is Life, the very Life of Life.
In its brief course lie all the
Verities and Realities of your Existence.
The Bliss of Growth,
The Glory of Action,
The Splendour of Beauty;
For Yesterday is but a Dream,
And To-morrow is only a Vision;
But To-day well lived makes
Every Yesterday a Dream of Happiness,
And every Tomorrow a Vision of Hope.
Look well therefore to this Day!
Such is the Salutation of the Dawn!

– Kalidasa

There is so much to celebrate in the world, just open your eyes and look.

Simplify your life by taking delight in life's smallest pleasures such as eating fruit straight from a tree, a baby's gurgle, listening to great music. Give yourself to life, one step at a time.

When you forget to live in each moment and are again living with attachment, which will happen, it is not a problem, just make up your mind to try again.

CHAPTER 10

Live a Life of Adventure

"Be not the salve of your own past, plunge into the sublime seas, dive deep, and swim far, so you shall come back with self-respect, with new power, with an advanced experience, that shall explain and overlook the old."

– *Ralph Waldo Emerson*

Do not allow your life to become dull by following the same old routine every day. Take up hobbies and activities outside your occupation that will fill your life with fun and adventure. If you watch a child, you will notice that with every new discovery there is excitement and enthusiasm. Restore your childhood spirit of adventure.

What is an adventure? "Ad" – means towards and "venture" means moving, so adventure implies moving towards excitement, enthusiasm and eagerness for discovery. It is to dare to do. It can be the simple act of departing from your routine and trying new things.

Adventures do not have to be climbing Mt Everest, riding camels through the desert or skydiving. They can be the small adventures you experience by trying something that will make your life more interesting. Think of these as mini-adventures.

Mini-adventures mean doing something you would not normally do to make your life more enjoyable and unique. Mini-adventures mean saying yes to experiences you would normally avoid. Mini-adventures mean meeting people you would not have otherwise met.

I recall a mini-adventure that turned into a fireside tale because of the unusual outcome.

My father, desperately trying to stop the theft of sheep from our farm, bought a number of ostriches, which he put in with the sheep. Ostriches are known to be good guards as they are inclined to be aggressive and attack strangers. After my father died, the ostriches were sold along with the sheep. Unknown to me, there was one huge male ostrich that avoided capture and so was left behind.

On a visit to the farm, I decided to go for a very early morning run to enjoy the new day before the rest of the family awoke. While running on a dirt road which meandered through the mielie fields, I heard what sounded like horses' hooves behind me and turned round to find that this huge male ostrich was running full tilt at me. Without thinking I dived into the long thatch grass growing alongside the road and quietly sat on my haunches hiding from this belligerent bird. He stopped right opposite where I was hiding, intently looking around. After some time I began to develop cramp in my calf muscles and knew I would have to move. I discovered an old mielie stalk within arms length. I stretched out quietly, picked it up and then, desperately waving my arms above my head and screaming, I leapt out of my hiding place and charged at him. Luckily for me, the ostrich took fright and fled. I ran in the opposite direction and only stopped once I was safely behind the camp gate. On my arrival back at the homestead for breakfast, the family had very little sympathy for me and fell about laughing as I told my tale.

My mini-adventure of an early morning run had turned into an adventure that is often told when friends and family are gathered together. While it definitely made my day more exciting, you do not need an ostrich to chase you to experience an adventure.

Be inquisitive about life. Join one or more organisations offering tuition in cooking, photography, running, canoeing or any thing that will bring spontaneity to your life. Have fun with dance classes or learn to play a musical instrument.

You might be afraid to seek new or unusual pursuits which challenge your safety zone. It takes courage to start something new but your reward will be laughter, fun and adventure.

Adventures need planning and time set aside from the routine of your daily life. It's worth it – for "The purpose of life, after all, is to live it, to taste experience to the utmost, to reach out eagerly and without fear for newer and richer experience" – Eleanor Roosevelt.

CHAPTER 11

Move to Self-Improvement

A person experiences life as something separated from the rest —
a kind of optical delusion of consciousness.
Our task must be to free ourselves from this self-imposed prison,
and through compassion, to find the reality of Oneness.

— Albert Einstein

If you are not in harmony with the truth of your situation or with nature then you are separate from life. You are living with delusion through distortions such as fear, anger, judgment, prejudice, expectation, guilt, envy, avoidance, attachment and resentment. If you are to live without delusion then you need to change the way you relate and react to life in all its forms. It means to see things as they are and to deal with them honestly and clearly.

~ How honestly do you face unpleasant facts in your life?

~ How well do you treat people who disagree with you?

~ Are you able to stand in other peoples shoes, that is, to empathise with them?

~ Are you cultivating the ability to see adversity as a means of personal growth?

~ How well do you appreciate and treat your natural environment?

Great people acknowledge their failings. It shows strength of character to apologise when you are wrong, to turn around and tell the truth when you have lied, to admit your mistakes and failures. Offering a sincere apology does not diminish you but makes you greater. To be fully human is to be willing to acknowledge your weaknesses.

Life is a mix of hope and hopelessness, joy and sorrow, success and failure, vision and disillusionment. It is not always easy. You will not always be totally honest in all your dealings, but strive continually to live your life with complete honesty.

By embracing the concept of *Ubuntu* you do not feel threatened by the goodness in others because your own self-esteem comes from knowing that you are part of a greater whole.

"Humility leads to the highest distinction, because it leads to self-improvement." – Sir Benjamin Collins Brodie.

Photograph by Siphiwe Mhlambi

"If you are humble, you are no threat to anybody.
Some behave in a way that dominates others. That's a mistake.
If you want the co-operation of humans around you, you must make them feel
they are important — and you do that by being genuine and humble.
You know that other people have qualities that may be better than your own.
Let them express them."

— Nelson Mandela

CHAPTER 12

Enjoy Simple Pleasures

If the sight of the blue skies fills you with joy,
If a blade of grass springing up in the fields has power to move you,
If the simple things of nature have a message that you understand,
Rejoice, for your soul is alive.

– Eleonora Duse

Life's simplest pleasures are free. These are the small day to day experiences that give each of us joy. If we can learn to concentrate our undivided attention on the small life treasures that enrich our lives then the love and joy that is inherent in their very essence will permeate our own lives.

A few of my own small pleasures are the sound of the rain beating on the roof as I snuggle up in bed, the smell of a rose or jasmine on the air, a solitary walk reflecting on the beauty of my surroundings, story telling around a camp fire and the shared laughter of friends, smiling across the room at memories shared with a loved one, the sky at sunrise and the evening star, dancing and giving my whole body to the beat of the music. There are so many small day-to-day experiences that we tend to take for granted. Simple pleasures have a universal appeal and remind us of how beautiful life can be!

Make a list of your own special simple pleasures and be thankful for them.

"Enjoy the little things for one day you will
look back at your life and realise that the little
things were the ones that really counted."

– Anonymous

CHAPTER 13

Become Abundantly Fulfilled

"If you want happiness for an hour, take a nap.
If you want happiness for a day, go fishing.
If you want happiness for a year, inherit a fortune.
If you want happiness for a lifetime, help somebody."

– Chinese Proverb

Martin Luther King said, "Everyone can be great because everyone can serve". One of the greatest ways to find fulfilment is to rise above a life of chasing success to a life of finding significance. Happiness comes from the certain knowledge that using your highest human talents to make a difference in others' lives makes your life one of fulfilment.

Umnutu ngumuntu nga bantu translates as "a person is a person through other people". The concept of *Ubuntu* is that you are who you are because of others. It is about a strong sense of family and community where people co-exist in a mutually supportive lifestyle.

With the world becoming smaller and families moving away from each other and away from their communities, many people are feeling excluded. Much of the malady in today's world is created by the breakup of our families and communities. There exists a remarkable culture of compassion when we are integrated into a family and community as opposed to living as isolated individuals.

The concept of *Ubuntu* still thrives in South Africa. It can be seen in the generosity of our people and in the sharing of all that they have, and especially in the giving of themselves when they have nothing.

A perfect example of this is the people who live on our family farm. These families are supporting orphans. The families say "The children are not ours but their parents have passed away so our home has become their home".

Thembe Majebe defines living with *Ubuntu* is the following way – "We live as if we were born by the same parents. They will pick me up when I am down, they will clothe me when I am naked and they will definitely feed me when I am hungry".

When you give from the heart and you are being truly human by giving, your life feels meaningful and you will feel revitalised. You will seldom feel isolated.

Have you ever thought where your money might go when you make the small gesture of paying a car guard for watching your car? The guard is taking home the money he makes in a day to his own dependants – to clothe, feed and house them. His job is keeping him off the street and away from crime.

If you do not have to walk the streets at night and sleep in the cold, if you do not have to beg for your food, or wonder how you will feed your family, if you are not out of a job or desperately ill, then your life is infinitely abundant.

> *"It is one of the most beautiful compensations of life that no man can sincerely try to help another without helping himself."*
> – *Ralph Waldo Emerson*

On a trip to Cape Town recently, I was travelling with Terrence Mtola and his wife, Zinzi. Having grown up in the Eastern Cape, one of the impoverished areas of South Africa, Terrence made the comment that many people they know are wondering how they are going to put the next meal on the table for their family.

Jostle yourself out of your complacency, for when you are serving others you move from self-centeredness to selflessness. If you give out of a sense of obligation or if you feel piqued about giving, then you negate the giving and can be left feeling drained and resentful. If you give from the heart then you will feel immense gratitude and be abundantly fulfilled.

CHAPTER 14

Listen to Music

"I sing my heart out to the wide-open spaces
I sing my heart out to the infinite sea
I sing my vision to the sky-high mountains
I sing my song to the free."

– Pete Townshend

People tell their stories through their music and songs.

Dance, music and poetry highlight the wisdom and beauty of African peoples. Music has also always been an integral part of any African celebration.

Richard Dowden from his book *AFRICA: Altered States, Ordinary Miracles* has this to say about Africa and its music.

What has Africa to offer the rest of the world? Patience, hope, civility – and music. If you judged the peoples of the world by their music, Africa would rank the most hopeful and contented. If music were wealth Africa would be rich. Africa gifted modern music to the world through America. All the rhythms of rock and jazz, reggae and soul have their roots in Africa. Africa's music is defiantly self-confident, irrepressibly strong. Life is good, the bubbling rhythms throb. Love life, cry its floating songs. African music expresses African culture more strongly than anything else. Walk down any dusty, litter-strewn street in a poor part of a broken African town and the thick warm air tingles with tunes like jewels threaded on a subtle silver wire of rhythm. Music mingles with the smoke of roasting meat at roadside charcoal stoves and the dust and fumes of cars and buses.

How can such irrepressible optimism come from Africa, supposedly the violent, suffering, despairing continent? If Africa produced the relentless rage of rap or the brutal speed of grime music no-one would be surprised. But there is not a whiff of stress or despair. There is no word for depression in most African languages. Africa's upbeat music is not some chin-up, always-look-on-the-bright-side pep song, nor an underground resistance movement, a defence against hopelessness. African music is hope. Its dances are life. Africa is ruled more by its music than its misery. Is there some secret source of joy in Africa that the rest of us have forgotten or never knew? Maybe. In Talk Stories, *Jamaica Kincaid, the African Caribbean writer, puts it like this:*

"Now, there are a few cultural traits that black people may want to deny (why, I will never quite know), but there are some that they just can't escape. For instance, they can't deny that they know how to make dancing music more than any one else, that they give better parties than anyone else, that they are better at dancing spontaneously than anyone else."

African music catches a spirit, a profound talent for living, enjoying life when it is good and surviving the bad times. The paradox is perfectly balanced: terrible times produce huge strength. Grief enhances joy. Death invigorates living.

Here you see death, disease and pain every day. It is out in the open, not hidden away as it is in Europe and America. At funerals the coffin is open. At the market animals are slaughtered with axes and the blood runs into the gutter. The beggar with stick legs performs his handstand in the street then swings his shrivelled limbs towards you – and laughs. The leper takes you by the hand. You will hear appalling tales: a lost identity card that cost a job and weeks of hunger for the family, a theft of five years of savings, an illness that cost a family its land, a sudden storm that destroyed a home and is crops, a painful death from an unknown sickness. Africa lives with death and suffering and grief every day, but to be alive is to talk and laugh, eat and drink – and dance. If you didn't dance you would curl up and die.

"It was your song that gave me wings
It was your light that shined guiding my heart to find
This place where I belong
It was your song."

– Garth Brooks

Music and song have a unique ability to speak to us. If you sit down and pay attention to how music makes you feel, you will realise how powerfully it can affect your emotions. Music is also recognised and accepted as a form of therapy.

Each day take time to listen to music that makes you feel positive and happy. Enjoy the feeling. Bad moods can strike at any time due to stress in the workplace, sadness from personal conflicts, an unhealthy diet and lack of sleep. A great way to beat your emotions when you feel down is to listen to music that raises your spirits. When you need a boost, listen to your old favourites – it works every time.

Sing along to music especially if driving a car in traffic or on a long journey. Singing along to your favourite songs will lift even the lowest of moods.

Engaging in music with strong beats and rhythms will draw you into the music and make you want to dance. Dance wherever and whenever you feel like it.

If you have a talent for music then develop your talent and give your gift to the world.

Music unites people, both for the listeners and the players. There is no better way for us to feel united and in harmony than through music.

CHAPTER 15

Discover Your Spiritual Path

"Just as a candle cannot burn without fire,
men cannot live without a spiritual life."

– The Buddha

Anyone who drives through parts of South Africa will be impressed by the beautiful churches at the heart of many of the small towns. They remind us that there was a time when people went regularly to church, mosques and temples and by so doing, derived moral and spiritual guidance.

Consumerism is our new religion and supermarkets and malls seem to have replaced our places of worship. Is it any wonder that so many of us live lost, lonely, empty lives?

If we live a spiritual life we are grounded and centred. We have guidelines with which to anchor our lives.

"Wherever there is inspiration, which translates as 'in spirit', and enthusiasm, which means 'in God' there is a creative empowerment that transcends the individual" – Eckhart Tolle – *A New Earth*.

In the unfathomable dimension of eternity, your life is as fleeting as a falling star. Take steps now to start living a life of significance.

Deepak Chopra is his book *The Seven Spiritual Laws of Success* says that "Success in life could be defined as the continued expansion of happiness and the progressive realisation of worthy goals. Success also includes good health, energy and enthusiasm for life, fulfilling relationships, creative freedom, emotional and psychological stability, a sense of well-being and peace of mind. Material abundance, in all its expressions, happens to be one of these things that make the journey more enjoyable. Even with all these things we remain unfulfilled unless we nurture the seeds of divinity inside us. True success is therefore the unfolding of divinity within us".

Matthew 7:7 says, "Ask, and it shall be given you; seek, and ye shall find; knock, and it shall be opened unto you". If you are feeling lost, read all that you can from the greatest teachers of spiritual philosophies. Your quiet time will be the key that opens the door to your spiritual path and will guide your way.

If you live with compassion and conscience and the basic values of truthfulness, purity, sharing, and non-violence with all living beings, then you are "with spirit", inspired, in touch with the essence of your being.

Archbishop Desmond Tutu was recognised and presented with the World Humanitarian Award. In his acceptance speech he mentioned that one of his greatest friends is the Dalai Lama. These two great men show reverence and respect for each other although they follow different spiritual paths.

Mahatma Ghandi said, "Religions are different roads converging to the same point. What does it matter that we take different roads so long as we reach the same goal?"

CHAPTER 16

Fascination Up, Frustration Down

"Everything can be taken from a man but one thing: the last of the human freedoms — to choose one's attitude in any given set of circumstances, to choose one's own way."

– Victor Frankl

It is natural to have times when you feel frustrated and times when you feel elated, but you can choose your attitude towards any situation.

Attitude is the way we think, act or feel about situations that arise in our lives. We tend to see the world from our point of view.

Learn to develop the habit of choosing fascination over frustration and make a conscious choice to reinterpret your circumstances in a more empowering way. You can develop the habit to stop reacting and start responding to the situations that arise in your life.

Think of our world as a garden. A garden needs sunshine, air, clouds to cool the heat of the sun, rain or water and the earth to feed the roots. A garden is made up of plants, flowers and trees. Every plant is unique. One plant may flower in the spring, another in the summer. One tree may offer cool shade and another bear fruit. No plant is the same as another. No plant is greater or lesser than another. So it is with people. Each one of us has unique gifts to offer society and each one of us has weaknesses with the potential for growth. Differences make us unique. The richness in our lives comes from the diversity of our people, just as a beautiful garden is made up from the variety of its plants.

By acknowledging your own faults and failings, you will find it easier to accept the weaknesses in others. The life you want to live is dictated by the choices you make. Being fascinated with a situation will change the way in which you look at it and how you deal with it. Frustration kills the soul. Life has meaning beyond your own small ideas and the key to true freedom is your choice of attitude in any situation.

My daughter and I will often use the phrase "Fascination up, frustration down" when we are faced with a situation that we might find frustrating. By repeating this mantra we are learning a different way of perceiving events in our lives. Even if there are a few things in the present that we dislike, there are still plenty of positive conditions for our happiness.

If you walk in the garden and a plant is dying, do not allow that one plant to destroy your appreciation of the rest of the garden, which is still alive, vigorous and beautiful. You can still enjoy the garden. A life of wholeness means you accept others with their flaws and vulnerabilities because you have these too. But you also have great strengths and beauty within so respect other people's differences.

Creating a life of beauty is a choice. If you can recognise that you are a part of a greater whole and are vigilant in your practice of good attitude, you will change the way you live your life.

CHAPTER 17

Transform Your Life

*"The value of a man resides in what he gives and
not in what he is capable of receiving."*
— *Albert Einstein*

One has only to look at life to observe how the world operates through giving and receiving.

As an example, let us take breathing. We breathe in oxygen and exhale carbon dioxide. The trees and plants take in the carbon dioxide and convert this back into oxygen. When a beautiful flower fades and dies, it produces seeds which, when given back to the ground, grow to produce another season of flowers.

Learn to give a gift to all those with whom you come into contact.

The gift does not have to be of a material nature. Give a flower you have picked, or on meeting a stranger offer them a silent wish of goodwill, a blessing or a compliment.

The more you give, the more you will receive as long as the giving and receiving are exchanged with heartfelt warmth. If you want friendship, go out and make friends. If you want to be loved, then give love and be lovable. If you want to be appreciated, then learn to appreciate others. The best way to get what you want is to help others get what they want.

Lift someone's spirit if you want to feel light-hearted.

"Transform anger with kindness and evil with good, meanness with generosity and deceit with integrity" – Dhammapada verse 223.

Because the universe operates through dynamic exchange, also be open to receiving. Receive gifts from others with gratitude. Receive the gifts that nature has to offer – morning sunlight, the shade of the trees, summer thunderstorms and the evening breeze.

The most precious gifts are those of compassion, appreciation, laughter and love. You can transform your life by giving and receiving.

"If we are cold, we find a way to get warm; we don't subject ourselves to more cold. If we are hungry, we eat: we don't further deprive ourselves of food. If we are angry, we don't fight it with rage; we try to be kind to this being that is suffering. If we witness evil actions, we generate sincere goodness and restrain any impulse to reject the evil-doers with mere judgment. To people who believe self-centred meanness is the path to contentment, we give generosity. And with those who are deceitful, we speak truth. This may not be easy. This is the way of transformation." – Bhikkhu Munindo, Abbot of Ratanagiri Monastery.

CHAPTER 18

Count Your Blessings

"Love cures people, the ones who receive love and the ones who give it, too."
– Karl A. Menninger

Dr John F. Demartini in his book entitled *Count Your Blessings* writes that "the connection between gratitude, love and healing is like a sparkling star of light, a perfect pebble in the stream of consciousness. When you apply these principles, you reap the benefits of healing your mind and body, following the wisdom of your heart and soul, and experiencing the most powerful force in existence – the power of gratitude and love."

My personal story of healing relates to the wisdom found within the pages of Demartini's book.

In my mid-fifties I was rushed in for an emergency back operation. One of the discs between my vertebrae had split and the section that had broken away was pressing into my spinal cord. I had already lost the feeling in one of my legs and if this fragment was not removed quickly I would lose the use of this leg altogether.

After the operation I once again read *Count Your Blessings*. Each day I recounted all the blessings I was receiving from having had this operation.

How blessed I was to have the love and care of a close family.

The warm wishes, thoughts, gifts and prayers of so many wonderful friends.

The concern shown for my welfare by my staff.

I wrote letters of thanks to the neurosurgeon and others who had assisted me in hospital and at home.

I also read inspirational messages.

I visualised being back at my yoga classes and touching my head to my knees.

I ate healthily and listened to my body.

My back started to function normally again and at my six week check up with the neuro-surgeon I admitted that I had started sitting and driving from within four weeks of the operation.

I started cycling and swimming once again. It felt so wonderful after the restriction of a back op. Within five days of being back on my bike, I crashed and destroyed my elbow joint. The joint was fractured into hundreds of shards of bone. I again had an emergency operation.

I was given a prosthetic (artificial) elbow and was once again incapacitated.

I could not believe that this should have happened to me when I had recovered so well from my back operation.

I felt frustrated and upset. I battled to come to terms with being dependent once again on my family and friends. It became difficult for me to maintain my vision of healing.

In those first couple of weeks I did not see any progress in the healing of my elbow. One day while I was looking through the collection of books in my study, I pulled out Dr Demartini's book *Count Your Blessings*. On re-discovering the wisdom in this book, I realised that I had allowed resentment and negative thoughts to hold back my healing. So I started visualising my elbow fully functional again. I wrote letters of gratitude to family and friends. I made a commitment to listen to my body. I listened to my inner voice of intuition and inspiration.

The diagnosis for this injury was that, at best, I would eventually have about 90% use of my arm.

Over the next few weeks, my elbow improved day by day and today I am 100% healed, both in my back and elbow.

I have developed a greater depth of understanding of my body.

Believing that we can make ourselves well is a vital part of the healing process.

I am truly grateful to have come to understand that the power that made the body can heal the body.

BLESSINGS

No journey you take is ever alone
There is always the white light
on the crest of your mind
The dove of friendship
always alighting
The whisper of encouragement
The beckoning stranger
To lure you on
or send you home
For blessings upon blessings.

– Bob Commin

CHAPTER 19

Dance to Lift Your Mood

*"We dance for laughter, We dance through tears, We dance for gladness,
We dance through fears, We dance for hopes, We dance supreme,
For we are dancers, We create our dreams."*

– Anonymous

It is very empowering to express your deepest emotions through the movement of dance.

Dancing in most African societies gives rise to emotions that cannot be put into words. Dancing can release emotions such as anger, frustration and sorrow and can be a celebration of life.

We all know that the way we feel emotionally affects the way we feel physically. But the opposite is also true. When you are moved physically, you are also moved emotionally. The way in which you move affects the way you feel, think and behave.

I have often come home after a long day and felt flat and tired. While waiting for the family to arrive home for the evening meal I dance wildly around our family room to some of my favourite music. It is not long before I feel re-energised and uplifted.

"To dance is to be out of yourself. Larger, more beautiful, more powerful. This is power, it is glory on earth and it is yours for the taking."

– Agnes De Mille

Facial expressions also set off biological processes that can make us feel either good or bad. Smiling and laughing literally make us feel good.

You can change your life by changing the patterns of body movement, gesture, and speech.

The bigger the movement, the bigger the emotions. Dancing each day to uplifting music will dispel your worries and lift your mood. Dancing is an exercise that is acceptable to all age groups, young and old alike, so dance whenever you can to your own choice of music.

Release your emotions and dance to music that moves your soul.

"We must not promise what we ought not,
lest we be called on to perform what we cannot."

– Abraham Lincoln

CHAPTER 20

Keep Your Promises

"Have the courage to say no.
Have the courage to face the truth.
Do the right thing because it is right.
These are the magic keys to living your life with integrity."

— *W Clement Stone*

I arrived at our farm on a Friday evening after a three-hour trip from Durban. I was keen to be at home for the weekend as there was a gathering on our farm. Catching up with friends, family and the local community at our yearly get-together was one of the highlights of my year.

On arriving at the farm I was confronted by my mother who told me that I was to drive straight back to Durban the following morning to keep my date with Peter, the brother of a friend of mine from school. Peter had invited me a month beforehand to join him on a date, which happened to fall on the same weekend as the farm gathering. Because I preferred to be at the farm I had phoned Peter on the Friday afternoon and told him that I was unable to keep our date on the Saturday. While I was driving to the farm he had phoned my mother and explained to her that he had invited me as his partner to his 21st birthday party celebration. When I called to explain that I did not realise it was such a special occasion, the disappointment in his voice was clear. He said "I wouldn't have expected it from you". I can still feel the sting of those words. I also know that they taught me one of the most valuable lessons of my life, which is the importance of keeping a promise. The next morning I drove back to Durban to keep my date with Peter and, because of having broken his trust, had a really miserable evening. By letting Peter down I reduced the value of my commitment and my word to nothing. I had lost his trust and damaged my integrity.

Even if there are consequences to saying no, the risk of saying yes and then not keeping one's word undermines trust, and this is hard to rebuild.

It is important to remember that in every thing you do, in every belief and in every promise you make, you are projecting your character. No one expects you to be perfect but the standard you set will be the hallmark of your integrity, morality and authenticity. Simply to talk about values isn't enough: we have to strive constantly to live up to them. Keep your promises for they are the foundation for success in your personal and your business relationships.

CHAPTER 21

Develop Good Communication

*"The basic building block of good communications is the feeling
that every human being is unique and of value."*

— Unknown

Life is lived at high speed today. Many people look for meaning in their lives by chasing the next smart car, the bigger house or a higher paying job with more demands.

The only thing that can bring true meaning to your life is to invest time in people.

Start with your own family and friends.

A rule in our family is that we always sit down together at the dining room table for our evening meal. That is a special time of day when everyone is home and we have the opportunity to communicate as a family. We have laughed together, cried together, had heated discussions, all at the dining table. This tradition has helped us understand each other and kept us together.

Good communication is absolutely essential to maintain close relationships within the family, with friends and in the workplace. Talk openly and honestly. Get your message across clearly.

Good communication is also about listening, really listening.

Really listening means sitting quietly and concentrating on the conversation.

Really listening means not having something else on your mind or being inattentive but keeping focused on what the other person is saying when they are speaking.

Learn to pay attention and be fully present while communicating.

"A sense of humour can be a great help – particularly a sense of humour about (oneself). William Howard Taft joked about his own corpulence and people loved it; took nothing from his inherent dignity. Lincoln eased tense moments with bawdy stories and often poked fun at himself – and history honours him for this human quality. A sense of humour is part of the art of leadership, of getting along with people, of getting things done." – Dwight D.Eisenhower

Archbishop Desmond Tutu has this quality. He also has a great sense of humour and the ability to laugh at himself. He is the conscience of our nation. He speaks the truth no matter on whose toes he may tread. These qualities are the traits of a great man.

CHAPTER 22

Become Unplugged

"Our world celebrates work and activity, ignores renewal and recovery,
and fails to recognise that both are necessary for sustained high performance."

– Jodie Allen

Have you ever been glad to be in a place where there was no TV, no computer and no telephone? The peace and quiet can be a precious gift to you and your family.

Electronic communications that were supposed to make your life run more smoothly and give you more time, now constantly interrupt you and in fact often prevent tasks from being accomplished and put you under stress. In the office there are streams of E-mails, instant messages and the telephone. Even when you are away from your office or your home, people expect to be able to contact you on your cell phone at any time.

How often are you interrupted when you are enjoying relaxation or are in deep concentration on a project? How often does the thought cross your mind that you would like to stop being interrupted?

Join the slow E-mail movement. The demand made by instant communication puts time-pressure on your life. Read your E-mails just twice a day. Recapture your creativity with the time to dream.

Join the slow food movement. Eating should be a meditative practice. Take time out to sit and savour your food. Many elements such as the rain, earth, sunshine and people have come together to supply your food. Your food is supporting your existence. Take time to savour every mouthful with awareness and enjoyment.

Quality rest time is essential if we are to remain healthy in today's frenetic world. Turn off that computer, that cell phone, that television. Besides your quiet time each day, find times to be completely unplugged. This could be two evenings a week, one day in the weekend or at least once a month for an entire weekend. You will be amazed at how peaceful and rejuvenating it is to enjoy uninterrupted time.

Our family has a small cottage at the beach. We made a point of not installing a television or a telephone and are blessed to have no cell phone signal there. We play games together, swim together, talk and also take time out to lie in the sun and read. It is an escape from the interruptions of our normal daily lives. It has become a special place where we reconnect as a family.

In South Africa we still have the privilege of wide-open spaces. Take time to step back and find respite. Make the effort to escape from your busy life where the busyness of doing can lead to mindlessness and an ungrateful heart. Become unplugged, find time to dream and muse and mull. Savour every moment and enjoy life with a grateful heart. Experience restoration of your body, mind and spirit.

Zulu people have a saying *Akukho nyon' endiz' ingahlali phansi* which means that there is not a bird that flies and never sits down. In other words – just as the birds take time-out from flying, so should we.

CHAPTER 23

Learn to Bend a Little

"No matter how poor a man is, if he has family he is rich."

– Anonymous

One of the greatest gifts you can give a child is a secure home. Partnership between two people is a relationship of give and take. If possible parents should be partners, with all that this entails. There will be times of disagreement. We need to make compromise a part of life if we hope for contentment.

Mutual respect for each other will increase as you recognise that you both have gifts to bring to the relationship. Honouring the strength in your partner gives him or her the capacity to grow.

Your partnership must be consistently linked to correct values and principles. The values and ethics that underpin your life will come through in all your relationships, personal or otherwise.

Create an environment where your partner feels free to speak openly and honestly and communicate openly and honestly in return. Acknowledge your failings and show your strength by apologising when you are wrong. Try to understand the other point of view and do not silence, criticise or humiliate. Share your fears and frustrations and celebrate your joys together. Learn to feel comfortable with these three essentials to any relationship:

~ Thank you
~ Please
~ I'm sorry.

Stewing over slights and hurts that are an inevitable part of living together can cloud your relationship for hours or even days. An apology before the end of the day will enable you to discard feelings of resentment before you fall asleep so that you awake to the new dawn with joy. Ephesians 4–26 says "Let not the sun go down upon your wrath".

Be available to your family. It is so easy to get caught up in other activities and to give your time to others while those who love you the most are put aside, simply because they will be there when you get home.

Celebrate any small achievement with fun and laughter. Life should be celebrated. When you look back on your life, it will be the fun times that come to mind and not the times of stress and sorrow.

You are not born as a good partner or parent. The amount of time you put into your relationship is the key to creating a good partnership. Your family's needs should take priority over your profession and the public.

"Learn the wisdom of compromise,
for it is better to bend a little than to break."
— *Jane Wells*

CHAPTER 24

Live a Full Life

"There is a time for everything, and a season for every activity under the heavens.
A time to be born and a time to die …."

— Ecclesiastes 3:1–22

Because everything passes and because everything has its time, recognise that time is a series of moments and that life can only be lived one moment at a time.

If you watch the news or read the newspapers, they are filled with stories of rape, greed, robberies, murders and corrupt politicians. If you reach out to people and connect on a personal level, you will see

that life is filled with warmth, compassion, hope and goodwill. Desmond Tutu was asked what he had learned from all of the experiences in his life and without hesitation he replied, "People are wonderful. It is true. People really are wonderful".

Life is about connecting with everything around you. Life is about nurturing mother earth and all she holds. It is about treating her gently. Life is about reaching out to the world, touching the lives of others, and making a difference in the short time we have on this planet.

Everyone says that they want to be happy. To be happy one has to accept that living a life means embracing all that comes your way – the ups and the downs. It means believing in yourself and accepting your life one step at a time, knowing that you are here for some greater purpose and living your life to the fullest.

No matter how beautiful and uplifting our ideas are about life, they are only real when we live them. The sun rises and sets and each day is

gone before we know it. Our lives are like a flash of lightning in the sky. Make the most of each moment and leave a trail for others to follow.

One of my favourite songs is "The Circle of Life" sung by Elton John and written by Tim Rice for the movie *The Lion King*. It reminds us that there is so much to see, so much to do and so much to be discovered.

From the day we arrive on the planet
And blinking, step into the sun
There's more to see than can ever be seen
More to do than can ever be done
There's far too much to take in here
More to find than can ever be found
But the sun rolling high
Through the sapphire sky
Keeps great and small on the endless round.

There are two ways in which you can live your life. One is as though nothing is a miracle. The other is to see a miracle in everything. Believe that life is a miracle and you will find it so.

Make the most of the miracle of your life.

CHAPTER 25

Get Serious About Delegating

"Business masters love what they do, do what they love, work efficiently and effectively. They delegate everything else to those who desire to do the same. To streamline the actions you take in your business ask yourself, "What can I delegate?" You'll be far more productive, energised, and inspired at the end of the day when you can stick to high-priority actions. Unless you value your time, neither will the world."

– J. F. Demartini

The secret of success is not in doing all your own work, but learning to delegate. This means recognising the right person to do the job. Delegating will buy you more time and is a training opportunity to develop the confidence and skills in the people working with you.

"Surround yourself with the best people you can find, delegate authority, and don't interfere as long as the policy you've decided upon is being carried out."

– Ronald Reagan

There are only twenty-four hours in a day. In order to live a balanced life where your work does not drive you into burnout through stress, you must learn to delegate.

When an assignment arrives on your desk, rather than take it on as another job with more pressure on your time, assign the work to eager, skilled workers who will handle and complete the job successfully.

Assigning work can make or break you. If you have not put in the time to train those who work with you and you do not assign your work well, it will create frustration and stress for you and your co-workers. The result will be an unhappy atmosphere. On the other hand if you have taken the time to train and create skills in the people who work with you, they will be motivated and your productivity will increase. This can be applied in your home and in your place of work.

Take the time to find the strengths in the people who work with you and develop their skills and training. It will be well worth the effort. You will then have the time to put your own creativity and energy into that which is important while others handle the rest.

CHAPTER 26

See the World from a Place of Non-Judgment

"We are all human — You cry like I cry, you hurt as I hurt, and you laugh as I laugh."

— Anonymous

When my daughter worked for a non-profit organisation called "Starfish" in KwaZulu-Natal, she came home one evening from the Valley of a Thousand Hills and said to me "Mom, if I had not been born into privileged circumstances, I could be an impoverished child of fourteen heading a household with three younger siblings, trying to feed, clothe them and keep them safe and warm".

How can we possibly judge others? We are all the same but for the circumstances of our birth and upbringing.

Children learn about the nature of the world from their contact with other human beings and the environment in which they live.

They learn about justice or injustice, they learn about violence or peace, they learn about intolerance or compassion, they learn about bullying or acceptance.

The world in which they live will often determine the lives that they will lead as they grow into adulthood.

"Judge not, that ye be not judged" – Matthew 7:1.

At the core of the human experience people are no different from you even if they come from a different culture, religion or are of a different colour.

If you open your heart and see the world through the eyes of others and from their point of view then you will accept those of different cultures and from different walks of life. You will recognise that they also have their own hopes and fears. Deep compassion, empathy and unconditional love result from a place of non-judgment.

Recognise the beauty in every individual regardless of race, social status, age, culture or gender.

"Instead of separation and division, all distinctions make for a rich diversity to be celebrated for the sake of the unity that underlies them. We are different so that we can know our need of one another."

— Archbishop Desmond Tutu

CHAPTER 27

Find Your Purpose

"Everyone has a purpose in life …. A unique gift or special talent to give to others."

– Deepak Chopra

*"It's the heart afraid
of dying that never
learns to dance;
It's the dream afraid
of waking, that never
takes the chance;
It's the one who won't
be taken, who cannot
seem to give;
And the soul afraid
of dying, that never
learns to live."*

– Amanda McBroom

I am married to a man who loves what he does and he has often told me how lucky he feels. He and I have always encouraged our children to find their passion and to follow it. Love what you do and do what you love. Henry David Thoreau once observed "Most men lead lives of quiet desperation and go to the grave with the song still in them". How sad to live one's life and to come to the end of it and look back with regret and a journey unfulfilled.

Life is filled with opportunity. There is so much of interest. There are so many avenues to pursue. But what direction or path do you take?

When is the right time to follow your passion? How do you choose and how do you know?

We all inherently know the answers but it can be difficult to gain access to them.

Often obstacles are external.

Parents, families, teachers and friends tell us that "you can't", "what would others think?", "there is no money in doing that", "you're too fat", "you're too short". Such obstacles confront us from childhood and often follow us into adulthood. We lose our sense of self.

But you are the only one looking at yourself in the mirror. You are the only one standing in front of you. In fact, you are the one blocking the process. To sum it up in three simple words "It's your life". We came into the world alone and we will leave this world alone and only we ourselves can be responsible for the life we've lived in between. Life will only truly begin when we assume total responsibility for it, and say, "it's my life" and plan accordingly. We are then driven by the pursuit of our own potential, rather by the opinions and expectations of others.

As a small child you knew the real you, you knew what you liked and disliked.

Bring passion, bring enthusiasm, bring love back into your life.

How long has it been since you felt that surge of excitement, that feeling of utter joy at just being alive? Make a list of the things you love to do, that make you feel good about yourself and your life. Look at this list in the morning and before you go to bed at night. Set a goal and only take on tasks that are aligned with your purpose. You can accomplish your vision if you believe in yourself and put your energy, mind, resources and heart into it, while at the same time, adding value to the world around you. Discover your life's calling. Liberate yourself.

Many times people are drawn away from their passion by the lure of money. Yet many of the wealthiest people in the world are unhappy because they have lost their soul along the way.

In other words, your aims and your actions lay the foundation for fulfilment but only if they emanate from your inner source, your consciousness, your intuition. When you live your life inspired by passion and enthusiasm and follow your heart, the reward will include money.

Remember the life you are searching for is not outside yourself but comes from within and it was there from the beginning. Until you know that life is inspiring, and find it so, you haven't found the message of your soul.

It was Socrates who said, "to know yourself is the beginning of wisdom".

Because everything passes we have the chance to start again in every moment, whatever our mistakes and failures. It is never too late to start again.

All things are possible.

Chapter 28

Become Well Read

"The book to read is not the one which thinks for you,
but the one which makes you think."

– James McCosh

Gcina Mhlophe, one of South Africa's well-known storytellers and authors, has a vision to make South Africa a "Nation that reads".

Gcina says, "In today's world, literacy and reading is the key that opens the door to the global village. Sophisticated computers and all sorts of forms of media are useless to a country that does not invest in the literacy of its people. That is why I am ready to dedicate my creativity and time to make a difference in the lives of rural people, particularly children whose situation might seem hopeless. I've been there, that's where I come from: Reading inspired me to think and dream big".

In a country with many illiterate people, Gcina believes that reading should be a vital part of South Africa's national growth. Storytellers can lend a hand in making South Africa a reading nation and it is to this end that she has travelled all over South Africa to perform, share and promote the importance of literacy.

Reading can hugely influence your own personal growth. Every person who is wise loves knowledge. Realise that you have a wonderful opportunity to learn and grow in knowledge by reading.

Take time away from the television and read.

Expand your mind!

Take the time to read biographies and autobiographies of successful and wise people.

Understanding the content of what you read relates directly to knowledge and wisdom.

Understanding is a step beyond knowledge. It is the ability to evaluate the knowledge.

Knowledge is the accumulation of facts. All that you learn in life is knowledge. To understand knowledge is to see the meaning or significance of that knowledge.

Knowledge is worthless if you do not apply it to your own life.

Books can instruct, inform, entertain, motivate and inspire. This is a simple and relatively inexpensive method of growing as a person. Drawing on the wisdom of the ages, books cover every subject you can imagine. Build up your own library of good books. If you cannot afford to buy new books, visit the second hand bookshops, join a library or start your own book club.

"Education is the great engine of personal development.
It is through education that the daughter of a peasant can become a doctor,
that the son of a mine worker can become head of the mines,
that the child of a farm worker can become president of a great nation."

— *Nelson Mandela*

Chapter 29

Discard Old Habits

"First we form habits, and then they form us. Conquer your bad habits,
or they'll eventually conquer you."

– Dr. Rob Gilbert

Life is a roller coaster of ups and downs, not just for you but for everyone. We all have good days and bad days. We all have times of being happy and times of being sad.

Often, though, we try to avoid the bad times. We look for the easy way out, and we build ourselves little "comfort zones" where we don't have to deal with the things that we find tough. We find a way to soften the blow, or to divert our mind to something else.

We have an argument with a neighbour or a family member, so we go out for coffee and a muffin. We are worried about a difficult day ahead, so we pour ourselves a second drink.

Little by little, these avoidance behaviours become habits, and mostly – like eating or drinking too much – they become bad habits.

Or we just go through life doing things the way we have always done them, just because it's easier that way. As a result, we never confront the challenges that could change our lives and take us to a new level.

As with anything that you want to change, old habits need to be replaced with new ones. The problem is that habits aren't easy to change. The bad ones hang onto us, and good new ones don't stick overnight. It takes patience and perseverance.

Acquiring a new habit is like knocking out a rusty nail and replacing it with a new one. Try, try and try again. As your new habit becomes part of your life, you will feel better about yourself and find enthusiasm for working towards your goals. None of us can travel into the past to make a new beginning but each of us can start today to make a new ending.

The potential for change is in your own hands. As you journey through life, it is inevitable that along the road you will trip and fall from time to time but you truly can embrace your flaws and failures and live a life of significance. Do not give up when you fall off the path but get up, brush yourself off and start again.

"The greatest glory in living lies not in ever falling, but in rising every time we fall." – Nelson Mandela.

CHAPTER 30

Create a Loving Home

"It takes hands to build a house, but only hearts can build a home."
– Author Unknown

A home that everyone gravitates to is one where there is plenty of fun and laughter. No matter the size or furnishing of a home, the warmth within the walls is what makes it a home and not just a house.

The first step in achieving a happy home is acceptance. Accept who you are and accept your family for who they are. Allow the members of your family to be who they are, without fear of rejection, criticism or continual advice. Accept their strengths and weaknesses, for we all have both sides, good and bad. If you fully accept and appreciate those who live with you, they will feel loved and secure and want to spend time with you. Allow that priceless luxury of unqualified acceptance to permeate your home.

There is a quote from a poem by William Ross Wallace that celebrates Motherhood. "For the hand that rocks the cradle, is the hand that rules the world." We are all enormously influenced by the person who cares for us in our infancy, most often that is the one who "rocks the cradle" – our mother.

Find occasions to celebrate your family's achievements.

Celebrate reunions by being creative. As my children grew I would make a special effort to be creative in welcoming a returning family member home. Communicate, pray, share and laugh together. This is the glue which keeps families together. Give for the sheer sake of giving. Motwa Ndaba says, "It is love in the home that builds it, and that is what makes us happy".

Remind those you love of their strengths when they are feeling low.

Understanding, love and acceptance are processes. They may not happen in a day, a week or a month. If you begin, you are on your way. It will take perseverance. If you fail, then try again and again and again.

One of my favourite quotes is "Not hammer-strokes, but dance of water, sings the pebbles into perfection" by Rabindranath Tagore. I have placed in my garden pebbles that I collected from the stream on our farm. They are smooth and round, having been shaped by years of water washing over them. These remind me to keep striving towards being the person that I hope to become in the fullness of my life.

By continually reminding yourself not to criticise and by accepting with gratitude all you have in your life, you will start to create a calm, fun-filled atmosphere in your home and your own inner serenity will draw people to you.

In 1976 my husband and I were lucky enough to work for a year in Georgia, USA. Mildred Cross, our employer, was a warm and wonderful person and this was reflected in her home. I copied down a welcome message that was on the wall in her family room and have kept it hanging in our home ever since then. It reads as follows:

Guest you are welcome here
Be at your ease,
Get up when you're ready,
Go to bed when you please.

Happy to share with you
Such as we've got:
The leaks in the roof,
The soup in the pot.

You don't have to thank us
Or laugh at our jokes,
Sit deep and come often –
You're one of the folks.

CHAPTER 31

Embrace Your Life

"Life is not the way it's supposed to be.
It's the way it is. The way you deal with it is what makes the difference."

– Virginia Satir

Live your life moment by moment.

What does this mean?

It means that you accept everything as it is, in every moment. It means that you dance through your life by realising that everything has a perfect balance. It means that when you perceive someone as being critical or verbally hostile towards you, it is an opportunity to look at yourself, grow and expand. Say to yourself, "What can I learn from this situation? What is this teaching me?"

When you allow others to pick you up or put you down by what they say about you, then you are buying into their illusion, their perception of how they view your life.

Your life is your life and does not belong to anyone else. Your emotions are your emotions and the only person they affect is you. You can create enormous emotional suffering for yourself by analysing and dwelling on the perceived negatives in your life.

The next time someone praises or criticises you think to yourself, "Thank you for reminding me to remain poised and balanced. I know you are in my life at this moment to teach me and enable me to grow".

Do not delude yourself but look at yourself and your actions honestly and see what it is that you can learn from a particular situation and then put it behind you. That moment is now past and you are living in the next moment. Avoid the mental suffering you will inflict upon yourself by re-analysing, dissecting and going over the situation again and again in your mind. Open your heart to all that life has to offer you and be present, really present, concentrating on the people, sounds and sights as they touch your day.

When you feel circumstances are against you do not wish them away. Accept the moment, just as it is, or it will lead you to anxiety and frustration. By simply being present and embracing everything that crosses your path, you will be opening your heart to a spontaneous sense of connection to everything you experience.

Every emotion has its opposite – like and dislike, patience and impatience, acceptance and intolerance, elation and depression. Everything is in perfect balance. Honour your life by looking for your blessings and your opportunities moment by moment.

Dance in the sunlight.

Dance through the shadows.

Embrace your life.

"I say love it is a flower and you it's only seed ...
When the night has been too lonely
and the road has been too long
and you think that love is only
for the lucky and the strong
Just remember in the winter far beneath the bitter snows
lies the seed that with the sun's love in the spring becomes the rose."
– Amanda McBroom

CHAPTER 32

Help to Build Bridges

We are "a fearful people, anxious about personal futures and institutional fate, concerned about jobs and security, nervous about 'transformation' and what it might portend, and aware of the fragility of language, custom and culture".

– *Prof. Jonathan Jansen*

The University of the Free State prior to 1994 was a traditionally white and Afrikaans institution.

In recent years the university has seen an intake of students from all of South Africa. Professor Jansen as the Vice Chancellor was asked by some of his students not to force them to integrate. This request highlighted how the history of South Africa has left people nervous, suspicious and afraid of those from another culture or ethnic group. It is up to us to banish the shadows that still remain.

South Africans have lived through one of the most dramatic political changes of the twentieth century and our biggest challenge is to bridge the gap between people of different colour, culture and background.

You can help build this bridge through making the effort to get to know someone from another culture or background. Honour the things you have no choice in, your language and those of other South Africans, the colour of your skin and those who are a different colour to you, your gender and those of the opposite sex. Accept the things you cannot change and the things that others cannot change in their lives.

Archbishop Emeritus Desmond Tutu very wisely said, "We can be human only together. If we could recognise our common humanity, that we do belong together, that our destinies are bound up in one another's, that we can be free only together, that we can survive only together, that we can be human only together, then a glorious world would come into being where all of us lived harmoniously together as members of one family, the human family".

CHAPTER 33

Fill Your Life with Laughter

*"The marvellous African laughter born somewhere in the gut,
seizing the whole body with good-humoured philosophy."*

— *Doris Lessing*

One of my earliest memories of being around the people who worked on our farm was their laughter. One day in the late autumn, a hare leapt out of the long thatch grass growing in the contour alongside the turnip field. This happened to be right near the feet of one of the workers who were helping to harvest turnips to feed the dairy cows. He leapt up into the air with fright. Everyone laughed and the laughter went on all day, as the story was told and retold.

Laughter is life's greatest gift.

As Charlie Chaplin said, "a day without laughter is a day wasted".

Did you know that laughter is used as a form of therapy for healing? Studies by Dr Madan Kataria of India, the founder of Laughter Yoga, and Dr Michael Miller, a leading US heart researcher, show in their research that hearty laughter can significantly improve cardiovascular health, reduce stress and increase work effectiveness.

*"Today, give a stranger one of
your smiles. It might be the
only sunshine he sees all day."*

— *H. Jackson Brown, Jr.*

Norman Cousins in his book *Anatomy of an Illness* writes: "I made the joyous discovery that ten minutes of genuine belly laughter had an anaesthetic effect and would give me at least two hours of pain-free sleep". Laughter and massive doses of Vitamin C eventually helped cure his debilitating illness.

Do not allow laughter to slip from your life with the pressure of our modern way of living. Even to smile at another will lighten your day. After all, a laugh is but a smile that bubbles over. Give away your smiles freely and in abundance.

South Africa is so lively in its diversity and so rich in humour that you can tap into it and rediscover your playful side. Rediscover the child in you.

Carry your smiles and laughter around with you, then spread them, they're contagious.

CHAPTER 34

Develop Ubuntu in Your Workplace

"Gratitude is not only the greatest of virtues, but the parent of all the others."

– Cicero

A number of years ago I decided to run a coffee and health deli. I asked my staff of six how they felt they could best contribute to growing the business. The consensus was that each Monday morning we would sit down with a cappuccino coffee to kick-start our meeting and discuss our ideas before the shop opened. During our first few meetings one or two of my employees, who had not had the opportunity to be educated, were very quiet and did not offer much. After a few weeks they began tentatively to put forward ideas as they came to realise that I truly valued and was grateful for their input. Some of the very best ideas came from these women, who were employed to sweep and clean, when they were offered an environment in which they could express their creativity.

Without realising it at the time, I was implementing one of the principles of *Ubuntu* in the workplace.

Mvume H. Dandala writes: "Ubuntu is not an abstract term separated from other things in life; it is buttressed and nurtured by life. While *Ubuntu* finds most vocal expression, and is inherent, in African culture, it is not exclusively African. It is possible for an African not to have *Ubuntu*, whereupon people might say *asingomuntu lowo* (that one is not a person), and it is equally possible for a non-African to manifest *Ubuntu*. The law of averages, however, suggests that, from an African perspective, it is people of African origin who are most likely to have *Ubuntu*. When non-Africans, particularly whites, show signs of *Ubuntu*, people might say *unobuntu ngathi ayingomlungu* (he/she has *Ubuntu* as if he/she were not a white person). Thus, *Ubuntu* is not something one is born with but that can be cultivated and nurtured by anyone".

It is often said that the best deals are made on a golf course, but through developing the culture of *Ubuntu* within the business environment, the ideas generated by sharing and learning could have similar results.

Life beyond the workplace cannot be divorced from your work environment, and if a business is to thrive then it needs to develop a culture of community and a thorough understanding of the people who work together. Many employers do not know that some of their staff might have had to get up at 3.30 am and walk vast distances to get to work on time. Often this person is the only one in a family who has found work, and by walking to work they are saving the taxi fare for other basic essentials. These people will arrive home well after dark at the end of their work day and still take care of the needs of their family. On the other hand, how many employees appreciate the responsibility of an employer whose business is struggling in a competitive environment, and he or she is shouldering the weight of keeping the business afloat in order to save staff from being retrenched?

When the values of *Ubuntu* are used in the workplace it softens the rigid, often hostile relationship between employer and employee. *Ubuntu* honours human relationships and how people relate to one another. It challenges us to become mature, generous and caring, and to embrace the culture of belonging and community within the work environment.

Most of us have almost infinite capacity for taking things for granted. I am convinced that if we allow gratitude to renew our lives daily, if we foster neighbourly concern, and if we shift from a material-oriented society to a person-oriented society, then we will see the dawn of a revolution of values where the highest priority would be the all-embracing good of all. In that way we would come to the personal fulfilment which many of us find so difficult to attain in today's competitive world.

"All of us might wish at times that we lived in a more tranquil world, but we don't. And if our times are difficult and perplexing, so are they challenging and filled with opportunity."

– Robert Kennedy

CHAPTER 35

Celebrate Birthdays

"Our birthdays are feathers in the broad wing of time."

– Jean Paul Richter

When my husband was about to turn 60, he decided to celebrate for the whole year running up to his birthday. He is the first male on his side of the family in three generations to have reached sixty.

That particular year has given us wonderful memories. We spent time with old friends, we celebrated with family, organised a three-week golf trip (his favourite pastime) and he and I took a special holiday for just the two of us.

Why should birthdays be celebrated?

Birthdays acknowledge our existence and our arrival on this planet. No matter the family into which you were born, you have one chance to live your life to the full. You are unique and your life story is unique. This alone is a reason to celebrate!

Make every birthday count by finding time to:

~ Sit quietly and think of all that you can be grateful for in your life. Your smallest blessings are often your greatest gifts.

~ Spend some time alone to reflect. Quietly ask your body to repair any emotional, mental, spiritual or physical damage while taking a quiet walk through your garden or the countryside, by taking a soothing bath, by treating yourself to a massage or lying and listening peacefully to beautiful music. Your body is a miracle and needs to be revitalised from time to time. What better day than on the first day of the start of your new year?

~ Be gracious in receiving birthday wishes or gifts from family and friends. Open your gifts while in the company of those who have given them to you. There is nothing more disappointing than handing a gift to someone who then puts it aside to open later, especially when you have gone out of your way to get something that will be appreciated. Remember this when you are given a gift.

Celebrating a birthday bonds family, friends and colleagues. Make your birthday a special day. Show you care by remembering and celebrating the birthdays of the people who share your life. It is a wonderful gift to make someone feel special.

CHAPTER 36

Patience Achieves Everything

"Let nothing perturb you, nothing frighten you. All things pass.
God does not change. Patience achieves everything."

– *Mother Teresa*

Three Cups of Tea is a book written by Greg Mortenson who, after a terrifying and disastrous attempt to climb the mountain peak known as K2, wandered cold and dehydrated into an impoverished Pakistan village in the Karakoram Mountains. This was the start of Mortenson's life mission to build schools in remote villages across the vast landscape of Pakistan and Afghanistan. One of the first schools he built was in Korphe. Greg spent all day on the construction site. He drove the workers hard. One day, Haji Ali, the chief of Korphe, told Greg that he was making everyone crazy and invited him to talk over a cup of tea.

"That day, Haji Ali taught me the most important lesson I've ever learned in my life," Mortenson says. "We Americans think you have to accomplish everything quickly. We're the country of thirty-five minute power lunches and two-minute football drills." Haji Ali taught Greg to slow down and make building relationships as important as building projects.

Three weeks later a landslide halted the jeeps carrying the wood up to Korphe. Haji Ali had somehow heard about the problem and the next morning a big dust cloud was seen coming down the valley. The men of Korphe had walked all night, clapping and singing to keep their spirits high, with each carrying a load of timber to enable the construction of the roof of the school to go ahead. This is a perfect example of how building relationships is so much more important than building projects. The relationships you develop with others will build your business because you have established caring and goodwill.

In our modern age, we have forgotten to build relationships because we are so driven by time and the need to get things done. How often have you put off seeing an ill friend with the promise to yourself that you will visit tomorrow only to find that tomorrow he is no longer there? Do you jump queues at the supermarket to hurry your way through the pay point and barely greet the person who is serving you, all in the pursuit of time?

Many of us in rushing through our lives lose touch with our "real life". We concentrate much of our lives on distractions instead of on priorities. Nothing marks the transition from youth to old age. It arrives suddenly. Don't allow your life to slip by you and wake up in old age with huge regrets.

*"The most sacred place on the
planet is Mama Africa!
The Swiss may have perfected the
clock but Africa owns the time."*

– Kingsley Holgate

Time is so precious. Focus on those things that need to be done. Spend the hours of your days on your priorities and put aside the distractions. Once you spend your days on activities that are at the top of your priority list, your life will change. You will be on your way to achieving your goals.

On the way to a family beach holiday in Mozambique my daughter, Candice, who was 21 at the time, read an article to me from a magazine. It described the rush of modern day living and she then turned to me and said "Mom, this article is describing you". I decided there and then to take off my watch for the duration of the holiday. From this valuable lesson I have learned to re-establish my rhythm with nature, to slow down and focus on my priorities. I have learned to say no graciously. If I don't focus on what is important to me, it is so easy to get caught up in other people's agendas.

There is a saying in Uganda: *"Ba azi asile si be ni yo"* which means, "No-one has teeth at birth". In other words it takes time for a project to develop, just as teeth take time to grow in a child's mouth.

Patience has its rewards. The things you achieve in a hurry are less enduring and satisfying than those you have taken time to develop. Take time to build your life story and make it worthwhile.

CHAPTER 37

Be a Good Friend

"I do not wish to treat friendships daintily, but with the roughest courage.
When they are real, they are not glass threads or frost-work,
but the solidest thing we know."

— Ralph Waldo Emerson

Loneliness is a feeling everyone experiences from time to time and it can manifest for no apparent reason.

What is it to feel alone? It is a feeling of separation or isolation from others. It is feeling that intimacy, understanding, friendship, acceptance for who you are, are missing from your life. People with low self-esteem often believe that others would not be interested in knowing them. This feeling of smothered, festering isolation can result in destructive behaviour such as turning to the abuse of alcohol, drugs, and over eating. Loneliness can also lead to anxiety and/or depression.

I can recall a time when I was newly married and had to have a minor operation.

I slept for a couple of hours and then awoke with a feeling of deep loneliness washing over me. I was alone and in pain. I remember longing to be back on our farm, where my mother would have made me a hot cup of tea, and would have sat on my bed, stroking my forehead as she had done when I was ill as a child until I fell asleep again.

I lay there thinking about this and came to realise that loneliness is nothing more than a feeling. I recalled some of the words uttered by Desmond Tutu – "At times of despair, we must learn to see with new eyes."

The words you use tell your unconscious mind how you feel. The words you use can either imprison you or set you free. The words "I am lonely" can have harmful effects because it is as if set in concrete. You believe there is nothing you can do to feel any different. But if you use the words "I feel lonely" then you are acknowledging that this is how you feel and you have the power to change your feelings. If you continue to say, "I feel lonely" and don't take further steps then it is as though you have opened the door to your prison but have remained in your cell. You need to step out of your prison cell by telling yourself that "I feel lonely but I'm going to do something about it".

Start by understanding a simple law of life, which can help solve almost any problem. This law states that you have to give away what you wish to receive. If I punch someone, they will punch me back. If I hug someone, they will hug me back. There is universal truth in the words "Do unto others as you would have them do unto you".

The obvious way to overcome your loneliness is to reach out to others who are lonely. Visit those who are ill or homebound. They will start looking forward to your visits. Become a friend by working on developing your relationships with them. Learn to listen and do not burden them with your own problems. Don't be needy as this will drain the energy of others and drive them away. Be a friend. A friend listens and in turn they will learn to listen to you. A friend comforts and in turn they will comfort you. By becoming a friend, you gain a friend. If you need a friend, you will find it at the end of your own arm.

Another means of overcoming loneliness is to invite someone over for a cup of tea or for a meal. Become more active in many aspects of your life. Exercise and physical activity will increase your energy and help you to feel better about yourself. Stop being a couch potato and do something! Express the feelings you have inside you by drawing, writing, painting a picture, or composing a song. If you're not sure what your interests are, just start by participating in various activities until you find what you love.

Join clubs or societies. That way you are more likely to find yourself enjoying what you are doing and being with people who genuinely enjoy the same things. You may also find out that some people like you for the way you already are. It was Tennessee Williams who wrote, "When so many are lonely as seem to be lonely, it would be inexcusably selfish to be lonely alone".

Telephone, write, E-mail or visit a family member or friend. Talking to an understanding friend, pastor or teacher is also a great way to dissolve feelings of loneliness.

> *"And in the sweetness of friendship, let there be laughter and sharing of pleasures. For in the dew of little things the heart finds its morning and is refreshed"*
>
> *– Kahlil Gibran*

CHAPTER 38

Allow All Creatures Their Place in the Sun

"This we know: All things are connected. Whatever befalls the earth befalls the sons of the earth. Man did not weave the web of life; he is merely a strand in it. Whatever he does to the web, he does to himself."

— *Chief Seattle*

Twelve year old Severn Suzuki made the following address in Al Gore's documentary film *An Inconvenient Truth*: "I am here to speak for all generations to come. All this is happening before our eyes and yet we act as if we have all the time we want and all the solutions. I'm only a child and I don't have all the solutions, but I want you to realise, neither do you. You don't know how to bring back an animal now extinct. And you can't bring back the forest that once grew where there is now a desert. If you do not know how to fix it, please stop breaking it".

An estimated 100 species are becoming extinct each day and a quarter of all mammals will be lost to our world in the next 30 years.

In the light of these statistics, becoming a "greenie" is no longer a trend but a lifestyle choice you have to make.

Any small service that you can do to slow down this process or save a species is invaluable, so switch off those lights, fix a dripping tap, clean up your litter and plant indigenous species rather than exotic ones.

Think of how we could not live without the sun and rain, the plants, which nourish us, our magnificent wildlife.

Take time each day to commune with nature in some small way, whether it is observing a butterfly settle to suck nectar from a plant, listening to the call of a Golden Oriole or watching the swallows collect on the telephone wires before flying away to distant lands.

Observe nature and you will learn to love it.

See your world with new eyes for you are a strand in the web of life and connected to all life forms.

Take action now for you cannot afford to wait.

Lawrence Anthony, a South African conservationist, has written a beautiful book called *The Elephant Whisperer*. Anthony, through bonding with a herd of "rogue" elephants, has come to realise that the animals on his Thula Thula game reserve in Zululand have taught him a great deal about freedom, life and loyalty.

He puts it this way: " … but perhaps the most important lesson I learned is that there are no walls between humans and the elephants except those we put up ourselves, and that until we allow not only the elephants, but all living creatures their place in the sun, we can never be whole ourselves".

CHAPTER 39

Let Go of Your Illusory Idea of Your Own Importance

"As a man thinketh, so is he."

— Proverbs 23:7

In the end, these things matter most:

How well did you love?
How fully did you love?
How deeply did you learn to let go?

— Siddhartha Gautama

What is ego? Ego can be defined as an inflated feeling of pride in your superiority to others.

To let go of ego, you need to be aware of it. Ego is the feeling of the need for approval from others. It is the need for power and control. It is the need to feel superior to others. It is your ego that drives you to feel that you must win. It is your ego that allows you to feel offended. It is your ego that drives you to have more and need to be right.

Your ego is your social mask and the role that you are playing and is sustained by fear – the fear of criticism and not being good enough.

Once you become aware of your ego, you are able to let go of your illusory idea of your own importance. You recognise that all people are the same but for their different disguises.

By becoming aware of your feelings, you will realise that it's your emotions that create your ego. We are constantly seeking approval from others. Witness it as it happens to you.

There will always be those who are brighter, faster, younger or more athletic than you. If you compare yourself to others you will always have feelings of being insignificant, worthless and insecure. When you let go of comparing yourself to others and you let go of

"By letting go of the ego and endorsing the efforts of others, good things will come in return. By giving, we can become better versions of ourselves. By helping others find their path, we're in essence reinforcing our own paths. And by so doing, we can live a more passionate life. But you have to make that initial effort to help others shine. Give it a try and see what happens."

– Lisa Hunt

the need to feel superior, you will connect to your authentic self.

Learn to observe life with detachment and you will feel happier and more content. Remain secure in the knowledge that you are who you are and strive to grow in strength of spirit.

When the time comes for you to move on from this world into the next life, the only thing that matters is the legacy of kindness, compassion and love you have shown to those you leave behind.

Sticking to the need to be right often breaks up close and wonderful relationships. Detach yourself from the need to defend your point of view. Nobility grows from disconnecting yourself from superiority, disconnecting yourself from being right, disconnecting yourself from feeling offended and the need for more.

When your inner resistance dissipates, you will find yourself empowered by life itself and will no longer be controlled by your ego.

Showing that you were wrong is not a sign of weakness but a sign of strength. Saying sorry is an act of humility and strengthens your bond with people. It draws people to you.

When you develop humility, people will want to work with you and will enjoy your company.

Nelson Mandela has this quality. He cares about others and is compassionate and generous.

CHAPTER 40

Retain Your Family History

"In every conceivable manner, the family is a link to our past, a bridge to our future."

– Alex Haley

With the speed of change in our modern world, not only in our own lives but also in institutions such as universities, churches and schools, keeping a record of your family history will help keep you grounded. At a time of complexity and change in our domestic lives it will give you a better sense of family and where you fit.

In a reunion of my own family, which lives mostly in South Africa, family members from as far as Australia, America and the United Kingdom became involved in researching and compiling our history. This gave us a great sense of belonging and solidarity. We were amazed when we were able to trace our family roots back in an unbroken line for 51 generations.

To me the most important aspect of tracing my family roots was the feeling of belonging to a whole, something greater than myself. It was a great adventure in bringing my own past to life, and finding my place in the scheme of things.

In societies such as the Zulu, Xhosa and other peoples of South Africa there is an oral tradition of passing history down from generation to generation through the clan praise. With the Zulu people this, the *Izithzkazelo*, provides an abbreviated history of where they came from, who they are, and major events and incidents that have occurred to them as a tribe or a nation.

At a time when English has become the universal language, by keeping your family history alive along with your mother tongue you will be giving your children an invaluable gift, something that they can pass on to their children, and their children's children.

You family is like the branches of a tree. You may grow in different directions, yet your roots remain one. Each of you will always be a part of the other. Do not allow your family tree to wither and die because nobody attends to its roots.

CHAPTER 41

Write the Script for Your Life

"I found that when you start thinking and saying what you really want, then your mind automatically shifts and pulls you in that direction. And sometimes it can be that simple, just a little twist in vocabulary that illustrates your attitude and philosophy."

– Jim Rohn

When we look at our history, we see that Nelson Mandela had a single-minded belief that South Africa could become a free and democratic society. He said that he believed in a country "in which all persons live together in harmony and with equal opportunities. It is an ideal which I hope to live for and to achieve. But if needs be, it is an ideal for which I am prepared to die".

Although he was imprisoned for 27 years, he continued to hold onto his dream and in 1994 he became the first president of a free and democratic South Africa.

When we strive towards our goals but allow fear and doubt to fill our minds, we have little chance of succeeding. Fear is in itself a prison. Real freedom is the freedom from fear.

Each morning I read from my collection of books of wisdom and timeless truths and apply the lesson from my daily reading to my life. One of my personal mantras is "I will judge nothing that occurs". Through repeating this many times to myself, I am managing more and more to accept that when things do not go my way they are shaping my life and moulding my character.

With this realisation, I find that I am walking through my life with a lighter step.

"We are what we think All that we are arises with our thoughts With our thoughts we make the world."

– The Dhammapada

Your body cannot differentiate between your conscious and unconscious mind. By repeating positive affirmations over and over you create your own reality. This in itself is a form of prayer or meditation and will take you in the direction of your dreams and the road to success.

We are all here for a greater purpose and by following each day a message of timeless truth we begin writing the script for our own lives.

We do become what we think about all day.

CHAPTER 42

Your Happiness Depends on Your Philosophy of Life

"The tragedy of life is not death, but what we let die inside of us while we live."

– Norman Cousins

"She was the sunshine of our lives" was an inscription on a tombstone.

If you dropped dead right now, what would your headstone say?

Have you ever sat quietly and thought what might be said about you at your funeral?

Have you thought about the legacy you will leave behind once you are gone?

In my late teens I spent hours wondering what life was all about. I used to look up at the clear night sky and wonder at the thousands of stars. I tried to visualise eternity. I watched nature and pondered how life could be so exact. The colours on a sunbird and the intricate weaving of a spider web, how bees pollinated the flowers and at the same time collected nectar with which to make honey. I felt an inner turmoil. I looked outside myself for direction to my life. I read books on self-help, philosophy and religion.

Over time I have come to understand that the universe is in itself perfect, and that each moment I live is as it should be. With this realisation, I am learning not to blame anyone or anything for my situation because any perceived negative in my life is serving a greater purpose; I am learning to let go of bitterness, defensiveness and hurtfulness. I am discovering the divine in all of life. I am following a path of no resistance and by putting aside prejudices I am learning to be open to all points of view, and seeing my life unfold with less friction. I am learning to love my life.

In South Africa we have people of many faiths and ideologies. Our conceptions of the divine and its role in our lives are varied and are determined by our culture and upbringing.

Treating people of different faiths with reverence and respect for their beliefs will unite us as a nation. The one all-important law that has been taught universally throughout history is to treat others as we would like to be treated and to live alongside each other with tolerance and humility. "Do unto others as you would have others do unto you" was preached by Christ. This was also taught by Buddha five hundred years before Christ. It appears in the sacred books of Hinduism. It was taught by Zoroaster, an ancient Iranian prophet, to his followers twenty-five hundred years ago. Confucius, twenty-four centuries ago, preached this lesson in China. The founder of Taoism, Lao-tse, taught it to his disciples. Muhammad, in *The Farewell Sermon* said: "Hurt no one so that no one may hurt you". It is arguably the most essential basis for the modern concept of human rights.

Too many of us spend too much of our time worrying about ourselves. We think of ourselves far too frequently as just individuals, separated from one another, whereas we are connected and what we do affects the whole world. When we do good, it spreads out and affects all of humanity. Lucretius, a Roman poet and philosopher, used the word universe in the sense "everything rolled into one, everything combined into one". So when our minds and hearts are open to receive all that the universe has to offer and receive it with gratitude and love, we will feel a sense of spontaneous connection to everyone and everything.

"To ignore people of other faiths and ideologies in an increasingly plural society is to be wilfully blind…. We are severely impoverished if we do not encounter people of other faiths with reverence and respect for their belief and integrity ….
In the deepest, most significant way, the goal of human life is not to wring the greatest personal pleasure out of every moment. The goal of human life is to live beyond the small, narrow prison of our own cares, wants and worries.
By learning to choose what is good and right,
we give ourselves the keys to true freedom."

– Archbishop Desmond Tutu

CHAPTER 43

Feed Your Family from Your Garden

"And he gave it for his opinion, that whoever could make two ears of corn,
or two blades of grass, to grow upon a spot of ground where only one grew before,
would deserve better of mankind, and do more essential service to his country,
than the whole race of politicians put together."

— *Jonathan Swift*

During our travels my husband and I greatly enjoyed cycling through the Umbria Valley in Italy. As someone who loves the outdoors, loves gardening and growing my own vegetables and herbs, the first thing I noticed as we cycled along the small back roads was the gardens full of edible plants. Nearly every home owner was growing herbs and vegetables in gardens bordering the path that led up to their front door. The food in Italy is delicious. I believe the reason for this is that the restaurants are supplied every day with fresh fruit, herbs and vegetables grown by the local people.

A generation ago nearly every home in South Africa had its own vegetable patch. In a country such as ours, where many people live below the breadline, we should all consider going back to the soil.

The soil is made for planting.

When you eat the food you grow yourself, you will know that it has not been sprayed with dangerous chemicals and pesticides. There are many books explaining how eating the right food increases immunity to disease and increases energy levels. Your body is affected by what you eat and drink.

The most frequent problem in establishing a garden is with the soil. A good way to start is to add organic material to the soil. Composting and mulching is a great way to recycle organic waste material from your home and use it as humus in your garden. If you are new to gardening then read and seek advice on the successful growing of organic vegetables.

Should you not have your own patch of soil, grow your herbs and vegetables in pots on your stoep or window ledge. Beautify your home with edible plants and surround yourself with the scent of herbs drifting through your window.

There are few activities more fulfilling than picking, preparing and feeding your family straight out of your own garden.

*"Much of the old lore has been lost, and patent medicines
have been allowed to usurp the place of herbal teas:
but at last herbs are coming into their own again, and we are
beginning to realise our folly in making so little use of them, and
especially of the sun-loving aromatic herbs. The mere scent of them
is a tonic, and even in winter their leaves give one a delicious
reminder of sunshine and joyous vitality."*

– Eleanor Sinclair Rohde

CHAPTER 44

Forgiveness is the Key to Freedom

"When you hold resentment toward another, you are bound to that person or condition by an emotional link that is stronger than steel. Forgiveness is the only way to dissolve that link and get free."

– Catherine Ponder

Many around the world expected a civil war with the transition from apartheid to democracy in 1994. Instead they got the Truth and Reconciliation Commission and they still refer to this transition as a miracle. Archbishop Desmond Tutu headed the Truth and Reconciliation Commission in which the perpetrators of atrocities and violence and their victims could tell their stories.

Many were granted amnesty. By unburdening themselves both victims and perpetrators were able to work through their hurts into healing.

Desmond Tutu has the moral authority, compassion and empathy that we should all emulate and believes that forgiveness gives us the capacity to make a new start. It is the grace by which you enable the other person to get up, and get up with dignity, to begin anew. In the act of forgiveness we are declaring our faith in the future of a relationship and in the capacity of the wrongdoer to change.

How can we not forgive those who have hurt, criticised or condemned us in our personal lives, when the leaders of our country paved the way for forgiveness on a national scale? There are people among us who have borne unbelievable suffering and yet are not held by bitterness or thoughts of revenge. They have transformed their experience into something truly beautiful and have developed a deep sense of love and compassion.

Whether you inflict harm or have yourself been hurt, both parties feel the pain. Both are hurt and need to give or receive forgiveness. Admitting wrong and asking for forgiveness restores a relationship. Forgiveness liberates us and sets us free and is rooted in making peace with the past. On finding the strength to forgive we transform from being victims into survivors.

When US President Bill Clinton asked Nelson Mandela why he had invited his jailors to his inauguration, his reply was "I was angry. And I was a little afraid. After all I've not been free in so long. But," he said, "when I felt that anger well up inside of me I realised that if I hated them after I got outside that gate, then they would still have me." Mandela smiled and he said, "I wanted to be free so I let it go".

CHAPTER 45

Live a Healthy Life

"Those who think they have not time for bodily exercise
will sooner or later have to find time for illness."

— *Edward Stanley*

A university student had an old car that had to be parked on a hill so that it could be started by running down a slope. One day the car came to a standstill and a friend of his suggested that the engine had blown. Being a student he did not have money for repairs so he put the car on bricks and for a year hitched lifts and caught buses to wherever he needed to go. At the end of the year he decided to get a mechanic to look at the car and give him a quote to have it fixed. It turned out that the battery was flat and at very little cost he had the vehicle up and running again. He was inconvenienced for a year because of a flat battery.

This story never fails to remind me how we can compare our bodies to that of a car. The battery of a vehicle will go flat unless the vehicle is driven regularly. The human body will deteriorate if we do not keep it exercised.

Exercise and stretching are the best way to stay fit and healthy. Performing physical exercise every day provides benefits to the entire body. This does not mean that you need to run marathons or be at the gym for hours on end. Twenty minutes of good exercise a day will be enough to keep you healthy.

Of course if you are participating in exercise that you love, such as kite surfing or playing a sport, then time will fly by and exercising will become a pleasure, not a chore. You can lose track of time in just taking a walk, absorbed in the beauty around you.

Exercise is the most natural option for helping to release stress so that you get a good night's sleep. It helps to restore bodily functions in a healthy fashion. Exercise will help you to re-energise. It will leave you feeling happy, content and balanced. It is not possible to have a fit body without performing regular physical exercise and eating well. Being fit also means having healthy thoughts. Your body will be fit when it functions well at all levels.

Proper nutrition, exercise and a wholesome outlook on life are the keys to health. When filling up your car, you are always careful to put in the correct fuel to keep it running. When you feed your body it is important to nourish it with the correct food.

Many of the books and articles written on nutrition give the following basic guidelines to healthy eating:

~ Eat plenty of fresh fruit

~ Eat plenty of fresh vegetables – preferably lightly steamed

~ Eat plenty of legumes, including beans, lentils, chickpeas and peas

~ Replace refined grains with whole unrefined grains

~ Snack on raw nuts, fruit, olives and unsalted popcorn

~ Drink water

~ Vary your intake of the above as much as possible to get the benefits of all the nutrients your body requires.

~ Minimise refined sugars, refined carbohydrates, fats and oils, animal proteins and dairy products

Ramesh Ramkumar in his book entitled *Being Human* says: "Remember that good health is not everything, but without it, everything else is nothing".

Tune up your body – it is the only one you have. Treat it well and it will serve you well.

CHAPTER 46

Learn to Expect the Unexpected

"To expect the unexpected shows a thoroughly modern intellect."

– Oscar Wilde

One of the blessings of growing up on a farm is that one learns to expect the unexpected. The most healthy and productive crop could be wiped out in one afternoon by a hailstorm, just before harvesting, taking with it all the profit for the season. A summer arrives without the relief of afternoon thunderstorms and crops and animals wither and die in the heat of a drought.

One October, in my early teens, the heaviest snowfalls in memory fell over most of East Griqualand. The ewes were lambing and because the tractors and trailers were snowed in, we rode out on horseback, with the snow up to our horse's bellies, to rescue the young stock in the camps. In no time the farm kitchen was filled with bleating lambs as we hand-fed them on heated milk and brandy to help thaw their frozen bodies.

'n Boer maak 'n plan is an Afrikaans expression used frequently in South Africa which means that no matter what the problem, a farmer will make a plan to overcome obstacles.

Disappointments occur when our expectations are not met. One of our greatest fantasies is the belief in perfection, such as the perfect partner, the perfect children, the perfect house or the perfect life. No one's life is perfect, no matter what might be portrayed in the media. When disappointment sets in with expectations that are not met, we are quick to apportion blame. This leads to unhappiness, both for the giver and the receiver. If we shift our mindset to look at the unexpected as a challenge and a blessing, then we free ourselves from the shackles of disappointment, anger and dissatisfaction.

Many a time when I have felt let down, I have made a conscious effort to shift my frame of mind and ask myself the following questions:

~ How is this disappointment serving my life?

~ What can I learn from this?

~ For what can I be grateful in these changed circumstances?

These questions will help to shift your perceptions, and will comfort and inspire you to get on with your life.

Being grateful for your life and the lessons that have helped you to grow opens your heart to unconditional love.

"Gratitude unlocks the fullness of life. It turns what we have into enough, and more. It turns denial into acceptance, chaos to order, confusion to clarity. It can turn a meal into a feast, a house into a home, a stranger into a friend. Gratitude makes sense of our past, brings peace for today, and creates a vision for tomorrow."

– Melody Beattie

CHAPTER 47

Liberate Yourself by Being Honest

"Integrity is telling myself the truth, and honesty is telling the truth to other people."
— *Spencer Johnson*

I have a very dear friend whom I love deeply. I told her the truth, which she did not want to accept. Her reaction was such anger that I instantly regretted having been honest with her. The hurt was so deep that it took many months to erase the negative effect of this conversation.

At its core, being honest is difficult because it makes you vulnerable. If I had hidden the truth or lied to begin with then I would have avoided being rejected by the person who I care about and to whom I had told the truth.

By being honest you are avoiding distorting reality and are assisting the person with whom you have interacted to grow and achieve. No allegiance or loyalty can require that you remain silent in the presence of injustice.

However, there will be times when it is wise to pray, meditate, deeply reflect and listen to your intuition, that still small voice within – thus knowing when to keep quiet and when to speak out.

"A person who wants to speak should think upon what he is about to say before he utters it. If it then shows itself to have some benefit to it, he may speak it; otherwise he should refrain from doing so." – Al-Nawawî

"We tell lies when we are afraid … afraid of what we don't know, afraid of what others will think, afraid of what will be found out about us. But every time we tell a lie, the thing that we fear grows stronger."
— *Tad Williams*

Everyone has the opportunity to make choices based on truth, integrity, respect, responsibility and justice. All of which develop character, as well as credibility and trust. All are the building blocks of high self-esteem and healthy relationships. Integrity is the choice you display in your everyday behaviour. It is the actions which follow your words and beliefs.

Being honest is a lifelong challenge but will benefit you throughout your life. Nothing is as liberating as having nothing to hide. Remember that being honest is not easy. Live your life upholding these values and people will consider your input as a valued opinion.

"God grant me the serenity to accept the things I cannot change; courage to change the things I can and wisdom to know the difference."

– Reinhold Niebuhr

CHAPTER 48

Don't Hang onto Grudges

"Breathe. Let go. And remind yourself that this very moment
is the only one you know you have for sure."

– *Oprah Winfrey*

There is a story about two monks who were travelling together. They came across a young woman on the bank of a river. She was wearing a beautiful sari and was reluctant to get it wet.

The elder monk said, "Let me carry you across the river".

On the other side, the woman graciously thanked them, bade them farewell and went on her way. The two monks continued on their journey for more than half a day when the young monk who had been pondering over this incident turned to the older monk and said:

"I thought we monks were supposed to avoid women. Why did you carry that woman across the river?"

The wise old monk replied. "I put her down long ago. Are you still carrying her?"

Do you carry around grudges, hang onto hurt feelings, mull over embarrassing moments and long for the past?

Your life is too unpredictable and fleeting to get bogged down in regrets and hurt feelings. Let go of the past and become one with the flow of life, whether this is in churning waters when your world feels turbulent or the quiet stillness of a pool when your world feels at peace.

Look at your life with new eyes and wonder at the beauty of the world. It was Danny Kaye who said, "Life is a great big canvas, and you should throw all the paint on it you can".

I once read that a man labelled an envelope "Waste of Time" and he would put negative and unhelpful thoughts into it and file them away. When he was away from his office, he would mentally file away thoughts that were not serving his purpose into this envelope. This freed him to get on with his life.

CHAPTER 49

Appreciate and Protect All Life Forms

"When we try to pick anything out by itself,
we find it hitched to everything else in the universe."

– John Muir

As humankind and human societies have changed, moving away from tribal or pastoral existence, people have become more isolated and have started to look inwards towards their own needs rather than looking outwards to the needs of the others and the world as a whole.

Everything exists in a web of connectedness.

An example of this is our deep concern with the worldwide threat of our diminishing bee populations. A virus called Colony Collapse Disorder (CCD) is infecting and killing off bees in their millions. The cause of this is not yet fully understood but pesticides and genetically modified (GM) crops with pest control characteristics have been suggested. American Foulbrood (AFB) is another form of disease which is killing the larvae of our bees. If the bees become extinct then pollination will not take place and our food will disappear because the bees pollinate the flowers that produce the fruit and vegetables we eat. One third of what we eat depends on honey bees as pollinators. The disappearance of bees on this planet would be a catastrophe.

A summary on *Earth Learning* puts it this way: To most people the word environment implies some object somewhere else. Yet, there is no environment separate from humanity. What is done to Earth is done to fellow humans and to the community of life that is Earth. The interconnectedness and interdependence of Earth's life web depends on a complex diversity of species to function as a healthy community. The human body itself is a complex ecosystem. Many of its functions, such as breathing and digesting, are assisted and performed by organisms that humans simply could not live without. Human outer skin often acts less like a barrier and more like a sponge. Just as a tree is not separate from the soil that feeds its roots, the water that flows everywhere inside and out, and the air it breathes.

In living systems boundaries exist for purposes of identity, not separation.

By trying to play God, we are destroying other life forms with a knock on effect.

~ What will it take to make humankind realise that we are destroying the earth?

~ What will it take for each of us to realise that in every action we take we can make a difference?

You have the ability to make a difference. With every action, with every purchase, you are casting a vote for or against Earth's life support systems. Consciously or not, every activity will either enhance or damage the Earth. Positive change will occur when enough of us embrace a new worldview that acknowledges humanity's role to celebrate, protect, and serve life on Earth and not erode its life support systems.

Your individual actions matter because collectively humanity can make all the difference in the world.

Freya Matthew writes: "What is wrong with our culture is that it offers us an inaccurate conception of the self. It depicts the personal self as existing in competition with and in opposition to nature. [We fail to realise that] if we destroy our environment, we are destroying what is in fact our larger self".

CHAPTER 50

Be a Mentor to a Child

"I believe the children are our future
Teach them well and let them lead the way
Show them all the beauty they possess inside…."

- Whitney Houston

Nelson Mandela said: "Children are the rock on which our future will be built – the leaders of our country for good or ill – which is why the rich potential in each child must be developed into skills and the knowledge that our society needs to enable it to prosper".

Children learn from the world around them. They emulate the behaviour of the adults who share their lives. Nothing can be more precious than the gift to a child of moral values such as honesty, fairness, respect, compassion and responsibility. It is a privilege and a huge responsibility to know that we are creating the future.

Children may gain an ethical foundation through the teamwork of parents, family, teachers and through interaction with other children. Every child also learns from cultures other than their own and may be influenced by traditions, histories, television and stories. A web of moral relationships may thus be woven into their lives and they in turn will become builders of integrity as they move through to adulthood.

How often do you get home tired after a full day of pressure at work? Do you find that you have given so much of yourself to your work that you have little energy left for those who matter most to you, your family?

Like most people, our family has friends of long standing. An attorney friend of ours finds the best way to relax and regain his composure after a day at the office is to change into comfortable old clothes and sit alone listening to his favourite music. Once he emerges his family can look forward to a relaxed evening together.

Many people find that the best way to unwind from the pressure of work is to go straight from the office to some form of exercise. A run, a cycle or even a brisk walk will do the trick.

Once you have recharged your batteries you can then give your full attention to your family, particularly your children. Have patience with your children especially when they are small. Try to make home life fun. Do not have too many rules but do implement the few rules you do have consistently to

"There can be no keener revelation of a society's soul
than the way in which it treats its children."

— Nelson Mandela

instil the correct values. Children grow so quickly that before you know it they will be leaving your home to live their own lives.

There are of course thousands of children orphaned by illness and other causes, who have no one to teach them moral values because they have no parents to welcome them home! An orphaned child needs to be fed and clothed for 365 days of the year but they also need to be loved and nurtured.

Reach out to just one child who is not your own. Help shape his or her future and so contribute positively to the future for all of us.

If you cannot take an orphaned child into your home, then support those organisations which sponsor and mentor our orphaned children. A child can grow into a happy, confident adult through the love and care of people who teach this universal truth – treat others as you would like to be treated.

CHAPTER 51

Live with Honour and Respect

"If one is seeking to build a truly satisfying relationship, the best way of bringing this about is to get to know the deeper nature of the person and relate to her or him on that level, instead of merely on the basis of superficial characteristics."

– The Dalai Lama

Guy and I made our marriage vows in 1973. Like every marriage, our journey together has had times of turbulence when we have felt distant from each other and times when we have felt extremely close. Our marriage has been a mixture of happiness, hurt, healing, resentment, gratitude, fun and laughter.

In looking back over the years I realise that the pillars of our marriage have been trust, good communication and the freedom to be who we are. There have been times that it has been difficult to speak to each other without becoming defensive. At such times, when there is unease in our relationship, we have written letters to each other to express our feelings.

By writing a note or letter it opens the space to reflect on that particular issue for both the writer and the reader. Once our emotions have calmed down we have then talked through our hurts into healing. This has been the tool we have used to move our relationship back into a place of ease after the birth of an argument.

Finding our way back from turbulence to peace is a journey required in every relationship. We all have characteristics that can irritate our partners and we constantly stumble over the same small, irritating habits. We are apt to repeat these failings, and striving to overcome them is part of the journey of a sound relationship.

In the western world, our literature, movies and the media portray "love" as romantic love or sexual attraction without appreciation and respect for the other person. As a source of happiness, romance on its own has a lot to be desired although that intense attraction or "falling in love" plays a role in bringing two people together. A relationship built without appreciation for the other person's character and value as a person is like building a home without foundations. In time cracks appear and the building falls down.

Any relationship that is founded on romantic love alone is difficult to sustain. Romance can enhance the bond between two people but trust, commitment and responsibility are the foundation stones on which a lasting relationship is built. Two people bonding their lives together share their ups and downs – and everyone has them.

Relationships based on caring, thoughtfulness, tolerance, compassion, good communication and genuine affection create a meaningful bond not only with a lover but also with friends, colleagues, acquaintances and strangers.

It can be the death of a marriage or relationship when we focus all our attention and affection on just one person. Marriage is made stronger by building bonds and relationships with others outside of marriage and in our communities.

As loving parents we have a commitment to our offspring that they have a loving community to receive them as they are brought into this world. No man, woman or family is an island. We all need the care of family, friends, community and neighbourhood to share our joys and sorrows and support us in times of trouble.

In South Africa we have a saying which says "It takes a village to rear a child." It does take a village, a community, to help raise a child, to support the family and help us weather the storms of life.

When Candice was a baby, my husband, Guy, who had already obtained a law degree, started studying for accountancy. He felt that he could no longer live in a society which was so unfair and enforced apartheid. He was looking to emigrate. Near the completion of his degree I was pregnant with Paul, our second child, and I could not face the idea of emigrating to a country where I did not have the support of family, friends and community to help raise my children. I could not tolerate the idea of them growing up without the support of grandparents, uncles, aunts, cousins, friends and community.

I dug in my heels and refused to move. We decided to stay in South Africa and in our own small way endeavoured to make a difference to the lives of those who were oppressed by the laws in South Africa at that time.

It has been one of the best decisions of our lives. We are extremely grateful to have the memories of a life in South Africa filled with the care and support of family, friends and community.

Marriage built on honour and respect offers the gift of a loving relationship between two people who are equal but are different.

"Love is patient, love is kind. It does not envy, it does not boast, it is not proud. It is not rude, it is not self-seeking, it is not easily angered, it keeps no record of wrongs. Love does not delight in evil but rejoices with the truth. It always protects, always trusts, always hopes, always perseveres." – 1 Corinthians 13: 4-7.

THE PROPHET

What of Marriage?

"Love one another, but make not a bond of love:

Let it rather be a moving sea between the shores of your souls.

Fill each other's cup but drink not from one cup.

Give one another your bread but eat not from the same loaf.

Sing and dance together and be joyous, but let each one of you be alone,

Even as the strings of a lute are alone though they quiver with the same music.

Give your hearts, but not into each other's keeping.

For only the hand of Life can contain your hearts.

And stand together yet not too near together:

For the pillars of the temple stand apart,

And the oak tree and the cypress grow not in each other's shadow."

– Kahlil Gibran

CHAPTER 52

Walk Together

"More than anything else, I long so much that we will become the country that we have it in us to become. A caring [country], not maybe hugely successful – we may become that – but one where every single South African actually feels they matter."

– Archbishop Desmond Tutu

We stand at a tipping point. A new consciousness is emerging throughout the world. You and I have greater power today than ever before to enhance or diminish the overall well-being of society. The world has become a village. With technology we are able to fly across the world in no time at all or communicate with anyone at any time, no matter where they may be..

Adam Kahane in his book entitled *Solving Tough Problems* tells the story about "a man who wanted to change the world. He tried as hard as he could, but really did not accomplish anything. So he thought that instead he should just try to change his country, but he had no success with that either. Then he tried to change his city and then his neighbourhood, still unsuccessfully. Then he thought that he could at least change his family, and failed again. So he decided to change himself. Then a surprising thing happened. As he changed himself, his family changed too. And as his family changed, his neighbourhood changed. As his neighbourhood changed, his city changed. As his city changed, his country changed, and as his country changed, the world changed".

Can you change yourself in a way that allows you to contribute to changing your country and then ultimately the world?

You are where you are so that you can learn to grow. Both pleasant and unpleasant circumstances contribute to your growing as an individual. You learn through both suffering and great happiness. You do not attract that which you want but that which you are. Good thoughts and actions can ever only produce good results, just as bad thoughts and actions will culminate in bad results. A peach tree can only produce peaches, just as weeds can only produce weeds. You can change yourself by continually changing the way you think. If you continually put an end to immoral thoughts and encourage good thoughts, then the world will soften towards you, opportunities will come your way and the world will reach out a helping hand to assist you in your endeavours.

South Africa is a microcosm of the world. We have dark skinned and light skinned people, we have the rich and the poor, we have eleven official languages and many different cultures.

Become aware of the impact each of your habits and actions has on the people around you and your environment. If you know your own strengths and weaknesses and you desire to live and work with joy and ease instead of living with fear, power and domination, you will have to choose your thoughts to shape your circumstances. Although simple, it is not easy to develop. It requires that you practice again and again to train your mind to be filled with thoughts of goodwill, compassion and acceptance. The opportunities to put your thoughts into practice present themselves in our conversations and in our interaction with others in both our personal and business lives.

There is a rising wave of awareness affecting everything we do in our lives, including our businesses. *Conscious Business* is a term used to describe a business enterprise that seeks to be aware of the effects of its actions and to consciously affect human beings and the environment in a beneficial way. Muhammad Yunus, the winner of the Nobel Peace Prize in 2006, said: "The World is crying out for a new way of doing business. When the social enterprise concept becomes known and begins to spread through all free market economies, the flood of creativity it will unleash has the potential to transform our world".

When you look at the world today, the one country that gives hope to all of humanity is South Africa.

South Africans can lead the world by pioneering "living consciously" as individuals, communities and in the way we do business. Many communities already practice conscious living through the implementation of *Ubuntu*.

South Africans have experienced some wonderful moments of pride and unity, a few of which are the euphoria of the birth of the Rainbow Nation in 1994, winning the rugby World Cup in 1995 and hosting the Fifa 2010 soccer World Cup. We need to entrench this spirit of unity – to join hands with other South Africans, pick up the baton of goodwill and pass it on.

There is an African proverb which says, "If you want to walk fast, walk alone. If you want to walk far, walk together".

By walking together, we have the ability to create a society where people are not judged by what they own or by the colour of their skin. Every individual will be recognised for who they are as a person, for what they have contributed to society, and for the actions they have taken to make this country a better place for all those who live in it.

We will live in a country where we will be safe, have a secure home, attend a good school and be able to make an honest, good living for ourselves and for our loved ones.

Appreciate, respect, love and be proud of South Africa's achievements, its national character and different cultures. Identify with other members of society and appreciate our cultural diversity, rich and unique.

Do what you know you must – in your home, community and in your workplace to build a future that was the promise of 1994. Do the thing that has to be done, because it has to be done and for no other reason.

"I truly believe it is our diverse nature that makes us a country of survivors. I am an Afro-optimist. We have come a long and difficult way and it amazes me that no matter what is thrown at our emerging nation, we still progress and prosper with every unfolding year."

– John Smit

Conclusion

In today's world we are led to believe that we are in a place of scarcity, no matter how much we have materially. Because of the influence of television and the media, we live our lives thinking that we are not good enough or that we do not have enough. We believe that we have been short-changed. We think of ourselves as isolated human beings, forgetting the universal truth of our interconnectedness with others. By diminishing others you are in fact diminishing yourself.

This thinking is in direct conflict with our African philosophy of *Ubuntu*, which has its origin in the indigenous cultures of Africa.

Ubuntu defines the core of what it is to be human. When you treat others with compassion, trust, unselfishness and helpfulness, and when you care for others and share what you have with your community, you are recognised with the words *"yu, u nobuntu"*, which is the highest acknowledgement a person can be given.

In other words, a person treats others as he or she would like to be treated. You are human because you belong, and by belonging you share and participate in communal responsibility. Your life then becomes significant by being part of the bigger whole. Nelson Mandela and Archbishop Emeritus Desmond Tutu are inspiring icons of tolerance and humanity and are the personification of *Ubuntu*, which is why frequent references to these two great leaders run through the chapters in this book.

Joy and abundance cannot be bought, worn or consumed, for they are a spiritual experience and are found in the spirit of *Ubuntu*. If you embrace *Ubuntu* then you are known for your generosity. You do not take advantage of anyone. You are large-hearted and open to others. You do not feel threatened by the strengths of others because your own self-assurance comes from knowing that you have your own strengths to contribute to society. You share your worth. This does not mean that you cannot strive honestly to enrich yourself, provided that you use your wealth to enable others to also improve themselves.

If we consciously harness the concept of *Ubuntu*, then together we have the power to step up to the true measure of our greatness and we will receive the most rewarding blessings of all – a life filled with family and friends, laughter, joy, love, peace and spiritual success.

Through the unity of *Ubuntu* we have the power to bring about increased harmony within society wherever we live, in South Africa or in other parts of the world.

Africa's Song

We are a people of the day before yesterday and a people of the day after tomorrow. Long before slave days we lived in one huge village called Africa. And then strangers came and took some of us away, scattering us in all directions of the globe. Before the strangers came our village was the world; we knew no other. But now we are scattered so widely that the sun never sets on the descendants of Africa. The world is our village, and we plan to make it more human between now and the day after tomorrow.

A.A. Mazrui (1986) – The Africans: A Triple Heritage

Dear friend,

In *You're Awesome* I have described fundamental values and principles that have helped me and many others achieve a happier and more fulfilling life.

If any of the lessons in this book have impacted on your life and you would like to share your experiences then please write to me.

Go to:

Website address: http://www.awesomesa.co.za
Blogsite address: http://youreawesome.co.za
E-mail address: di@awesomesa.co.za

P.O. Box 13111,
Cascades
Pietermartizburg
3202
KwaZulu-Natal
South Africa

May you live with joy and peace.

Love and best wishes,
Di Smith